Praise for *ELL Fro......*

This book will show you how to embrace technology and harness its power to meet the needs of your students. In the era of data-driven instruction and the need for differentiation for the diverse needs of ELs in the classroom, a technology-rich learning environment provides the opportunity to deliver lessons that allow for the precious time in class to be spent completing hands-on activities and using English in an authentic and meaningful manner.

—Mandi Sanchez
Mid-State RBERN (Regional Bilingual Education
Resource Network)
Liverpool, NY

The effective and purposeful use of technology tools can have a powerful impact on collaboration and the successful implementation of co-teaching models to best support English Learners. This book will help you to use technology tools that allow ELs to more fully participate with their peers. This will positively impact on learning and growth of the student. Through the effective use of technology tools, the important learning happening in the classroom will also be positively impacted.

—Paul Louis
Director of Curriculum and Assessment
Kildeer School District 96

Many of our students are digital natives, no matter what their proficiency in English is! Since each author has worked directly with ELLs, their expertise is reflected in the tips they offer. This text will provide not only a hands-on guidebook for how to use technology specifically for our ELLs, but also the research to support each strategy provided. A must-read in our linguistically diverse, digital-age learning environments today!

—Susanne Marcus
NYS TESOL Past President

The ideas introduced in this book can assist us in making the most of the available technology and digital resources of our 21st century classrooms as we plan instruction with our curriculum. The information is presented in an accessible and engaging way to regularly incorporate students' lived experiences and the authentic phenomena of their world—through content using visual texts, videos, and other digital resources. This book can guide us to make the most of our face-to-face time with students through rich tasks requiring higher-level thinking and application of learning. Additionally, the "seed" lessons provide us with powerful entry points that support integration of the flipped classroom approach into our practice such that we may promote academic equity for ELLs and all learners.

—Zaiba Beg
Instructional Coordinator: English Language
Learners, ESL/ELB programs
Peel District School Board

Parris, Estrada, and Honigsfeld offer a dynamic reinterpretation of the learning and teaching environment in their book ELL Frontiers. *With attention to detail, they describe learning possibilities and how technology can support English learners' mastery of academic vocabulary and concepts, their development of oral fluency, and their participation in creative teams with native English-speaking students for mutual growth and benefit. Teachers will flip (with joy) as they read the many ways they can support ELs with technology and how such a classroom can promote authentic learning and assessment.*

—Don Hones
Chair of Department of Teaching and Learning
University of Wisconsin, Osh Kosh

A much-needed book to empower educators to empower their English language learners! ELL Frontiers *contains tools and resources that narrow the digital divide and put students at the center, fostering active learning, as well as independent and engaged learners. New and experienced educators alike will learn what technology can do for the English language learner as a citizen of the digital age.*

—Carolyn Frye
ELL Resource Teacher, English Language Learners Services
Charlotte-Mecklenburg Schools

Digital teaching is an important resource for supporting and enhancing learning for all students, yet it has not been the focus of many professional resource books for working with second-language learners. ELL Frontiers: Using Technology to Enhance Instruction for English Learners *changes that. Finally, here is a source for teachers who work with English learners that provides innovative, thoughtful, and clearly articulated ideas for actively involving students in digital learning using the latest technology while keeping in mind best practices for collaborating, conversing, and providing feedback in the classroom. The authors share a range of approaches that help students bolster their background knowledge, think critically, and use class time to interact and engage, such as through flipping the classroom. This book contains a treasure trove of ideas for teachers who want to move their teaching with English learners into the digital age.*

—Lori Helman, PhD
Director, Minnesota Center for Reading Research
Associate Professor, Literacy Education
University of Minnesota

High praise to Parris, Estrada, and Honigsfeld for providing this timely contribution to all of us involved in educating one of the nation's fastest growing populations. Teachers, administrators, and specialists, as well as curriculum and professional development leaders will find a treasure trove of strategies and research-based solutions for teaching English learners during our rapidly evolving digital era.

—Debbie Zacarian, EdD
debbie@zacarianconsulting.com
zacarianconsulting.com

Parris, Estrada, and Honigsfeld have brought important attention to English learners (ELs) as digital learners. This is the first book I have seen to provide support for educators as they are increasingly required to implement technology with diverse learners. The text is practical and provides encouragement for educators who are often just learning the technology themselves. This book is structured to provide teachers with valuable information on different tech tools and teaching methods, a discussion of how to scaffold for ELs, the strengths and challenges; as well as authentic examples for readers to reflect on and build upon with their own ideas.

—Kristina Robertson, English Learners
Program Administrator
Roseville Area Schools, Roseville, MN

ELL Frontiers

ELL Frontiers

Using Technology to Enhance Instruction for English Learners

Heather Parris
Lisa Estrada
Andrea Honigsfeld

Foreword by Jon Bergmann

CORWIN
A SAGE Publishing Company

FOR INFORMATION:

Corwin

A SAGE Company

2455 Teller Road

Thousand Oaks, California 91320

(800) 233-9936

www.corwin.com

SAGE Publications Ltd.

1 Oliver's Yard

55 City Road

London EC1Y 1SP

United Kingdom

SAGE Publications India Pvt. Ltd.

B 1/I 1 Mohan Cooperative Industrial Area

Mathura Road, New Delhi 110 044

India

SAGE Publications Asia-Pacific Pte. Ltd.

3 Church Street

#10-04 Samsung Hub

Singapore 049483

Program Director: Dan Alpert

Senior Associate Editor: Kimberly Greenberg

Editorial Assistant: Katie Crilley

Production Editor: Amy Schroller

Copy Editor: Mark Bast

Typesetter: C&M Digitals (P) Ltd.

Proofreader: Dennis W. Webb

Indexer: Sheila Bodell

Cover Designer: Gail Buschman

Marketing Manager: Charline Maher

Printed in the United States of America

Library of Congress Cataloging-in-Publication Data

Names: Parris, Heather, author. | Estrada, Lisa, author. | Honigsfeld, Andrea M., author.

Title: ESL frontiers : using technology to enhance instruction for English learners / Heather Parris, Lisa Estrada, Andrea M. Honigsfeld.

Description: Thousand Oaks, California. : Corwin, [2016] | Includes bibliographical references and index.

Identifiers: LCCN 2016021881 | ISBN 9781506315089 (pbk. : alk. paper)

Subjects: LCSH: English language—Study and teaching—Technological innovations. | English language—Study and teaching—Computer-assisted instruction. | English teachers—Training of. | English language—Computer network resources. | Language and languages—Study and teaching. | Second language acqusition | Applied linguistics.

Classification: LCC PE1128.A2 P325 2016 | DDC 428.0078—dc23 LC record available at https://lccn.loc.gov/2016021881

This book is printed on acid-free paper.

SFI® Certified Sourcing
www.sfiprogram.org
SFI-00453

16 17 18 19 20 10 9 8 7 6 5 4 3 2 1

Contents

Foreword

I was perusing poster sessions at the 2014 ISTE conference, and came across one by Heather and Lisa. They were sharing about how they were flipping instruction for ELLs and I was intrigued. As we were chatting, I realized that they were some of the first to contextualize flipped learning for ELL students. As they looked at the daily challenges their students face, they realized that they must adapt to meet each student's needs. Their thinking outside the box with an innovative mindset is something the world of education needs.

The world has changed. Most of us veteran teachers grew up in a time when information was scarce. We acquired knowledge from libraries, textbooks, or through the expertise of our teachers. Contrast this with the present day where information is easy to access; an information-saturated world. Now the challenge is not to get information, but rather to filter all of the information and determine what is valid and what is not. There are those who feel that technology will transform education, so they have thrown devices at schools in an attempt to achieve that. Sadly, this has not occurred because some of these innovators have things backward. They start with the technology and then add pedagogy on top. The reality is that we must start with good pedagogy and then add technology where it is most needed.

What I appreciate about Heather, Lisa, and Andrea is that they get it! They are starting with good pedagogy and are making appropriate connections to sound technology. Their commitment to the art and craft of teaching comes first, and the implementation of technology second.

What you will find in this book is a rich discussion of sound pedagogy coupled with the ways that technology enhances the teaching of English learners. They dive deep into communication, critical thinking, creativity, collaboration, and assessment. This work is an excellent addition to any teacher's library. It is both practical and aspirational. It will challenge you to think differently about the teaching of ELLs and at the same time validate some of what you have already known about a quality education.

Read on!

Jon Bergmann
Teacher, Author, and Flipped Learning Pioneer
jonbergmann.com

Publisher's Acknowledgments

Corwin gratefully acknowledges the contributions of the following reviewers:

Erin Taylor Dougherty
ESOL Teacher
Louisa County Public Schools
Mineral, VA

Jane Holmberg, EdD
Educational Consultant
Uncommon Leadership
Mound, MN

Sandy Kluver
ESL Instructor
Carroll Community School District
Carroll, IA

Linda Lippitt, PhD
ESL/Migrant Education Director
Henderson County Public Schools
Hendersonville, NC

Lori Menning
ELL/Bilingual Instructor
School District of New London
Neenah, WI

About the Authors

Heather Parris is the cofounder of Estrada & Parris, LLC, an educational consulting group that provides professional development and curriculum design on instructional strategies and technology integration for the K–12 classroom. She has over 20 years of experience in both K–12 and higher education settings and is currently an adjunct professor for the Molloy College Graduate School of Education in Rockville Centre, New York. As coauthor of the blog esltechies.com, she shares her passion for edtech and English language development. Her combined expertise on ELs (English learners) and the use of technology to support learning developed while working for the Board of Cooperative Educational Services of Nassau County (Nassau BOCES), where she was first an ESL program specialist for the NYSED Bilingual/ESL Technical Assistance Center and then the program coordinator of Model Schools/Digital Age Teaching and Education. She conducts workshops and presents regularly at regional, national, and international conferences. She was a contributor and section editor for the NYSED (2011) *Guidelines for Educating Limited English Proficient Students With Interrupted Formal Education.*

She holds a master's of science in education degree for teaching English to speakers of other languages from Queens College, City University of New York, and a professional diploma in school district leadership from Fordham University.

Lisa Estrada is the supervisor of English as a new language (ENL) and world languages at Hicksville Public Schools in Hicksville, New York. She is also an adjunct professor in the Molloy College Clinically-Rich Intensive Teacher Institute in Rockville Centre, New York. Her educational experience and training includes over 25 years of ESL and bilingual education in K–12 settings, as well as many years as an ESL/bilingual program coordinator for the Board of Cooperative Educational Services of Nassau County (Nassau BOCES). She conducts workshops and presents regularly at regional, national, and international conferences.

In 2011, she was a contributor and section editor for the NYSED *Guidelines for Educating Limited English Proficient Students With Interrupted Formal Education.* She coauthors esltechies.com, a blog dedicated to providing free instructional resources to teachers of English learners. She is also the cofounder of Estrada & Parris, LLC, a privately owned educational consulting group that provides professional development and curriculum design on instructional strategies and technology integration for the K–12 classroom. She holds a master's of arts degree in teaching English to speakers of other languages with a bilingual extension from Adelphi University. She also holds a professional diploma in school administration from Long Island University/C.W. Post.

Andrea Honigsfeld, EdD, is an associate dean and director of the Educational Leadership for Diverse Learning Communities doctoral program in the Division of Education at Molloy College, Rockville Centre, New York. Before entering the field of teacher education, she was an English-as-a-foreign-language teacher in Hungary (Grades 5–8 and adult) and an English-as-a-second-language teacher in New York City (Grades K–3 and adult). She also taught Hungarian at New York University.

She was the recipient of a doctoral fellowship at St. John's University, where she conducted research on individualized instruction and learning styles. She has published extensively on working with English learners and providing individualized instruction based on learning style preferences. She received a Fulbright Award to lecture in Iceland in the fall of 2002. In the past 12 years, she has presented at conferences across the United States, Great Britain, Denmark, Sweden, the Philippines, and the United Arab Emirates. She frequently offers staff development primarily focusing on effective differentiated literacy strategies and collaborative practices for English-as-a-second-language and general-education teachers. This is her sixth Corwin book, all others coauthored with Maria G. Dove or Audrey Cohan.

To Holly, Liam, and Emily— for forgoing home cooked meals.
I love you forever, I like you for always.
To Eric—for sitting with me while I wrote.
Thank you for your constant encouragement. I love you
with all my heart.— HP

In loving memory of my mother
whose spirit sustains me and serves as my inspiration.
To my family, thank you for all of your love, support, and faith in me.
You mean the world to me!—LE

To Howie, Ben, Jacob, and Noah—your support means
the world to me.—AH

1
The 21st Century English Learner

The skills and knowledge needed to be successful today are different from those needed fifty, twenty, or even ten years ago. As the global marketplace rapidly evolves, the landscape of education must also evolve to adequately prepare students for life beyond secondary school. (Tucker, 2012, p. 3)

THE DIGITAL AGE ELD/ESL CLASSROOM

English language development (ELD) programs and English as a second language (ESL) methodology has evolved over the years from a variety of practices starting with no model at all, as in the "sink or swim" method, to grammar translation, the audio-lingual method, total physical response (TPR), and the sheltered instruction observation protocol (SIOP), to name a few. Each methodology improved on previous strategies to better assist English learners (ELs) achieve proficiency. Today, with the arrival of the digital age, it has become necessary to reexamine the delivery of ELD/ESL instruction once again, in order to provide our students with 21st century skills and experiences. It is important as teachers of ELs to ask, what exactly is 21st century learning, and how are we preparing ELs to participate in this new educational environment? In this book we examine current understandings of digital age education and explore how we can improve instructional methodology for English learners to meet the demands of this new classroom era.

In order to clarify what 21st century learning encompasses, the Partnership for 21st Century Learning (P21) provides all educators with discrete skills that students are expected to acquire in order to participate successfully in the fast-paced, globally oriented digital age. Let's take a

look at the outcomes described from the P21 framework (http://www
.p21.org/our-work/p21-framework) and how they may relate to ELs:

1. *Content knowledge and 21st century themes*. In addition to essential
   core content knowledge in traditional subject areas such as English,
   world languages, mathematics, science, social studies, and art, the
   framework includes the integration of 21st century themes such as
   global awareness; environmental, health, and civic literacy; and
   financial, economic, business, and entrepreneurial literacy. This
   blend of content knowledge and literacies requires that we provide
   ELs with a skills base that far exceeds previous academic, cultural,
   and linguistic demands.

2. *Learning and innovation skills*. These are the skills that separate today's
   learner from the past and assist them in navigating our complex digital age. The emphasis is on the 4 C's: creativity, critical thinking, communication, and collaboration. In this book, we add and discuss a
   fifth "C" for culture, in order to raise global awareness and the need
   to address diversity and multiculturalism in the classroom.

3. *Information, media, and technology skills*. Information and communication technology literacy (ICT) must be integrated into core subject
   areas and includes a student's ability to create, assess, and apply
   information and digital media effectively. This also includes understanding and using the most current technology tools. For ELs we
   must always be mindful of the digital divide that currently exists
   between communities of learners and work diligently to pursue
   equitable access to digital resources for our students.

4. *Life and career skills*. The final student outcome included in the P21
   framework recognizes the need to develop a student's socioemotional skills in conjunction with core content knowledge. Topics
   included in this theme include flexibility and adaptation, productivity and accountability, initiative and self-direction, leadership and
   responsibility, and social and cross-cultural skills. English learners
   often come to this country with acute socioemotional needs related to
   the cross-cultural transition they are experiencing and require
   additional assistance to navigate the life and career skills mentioned.

ENGLISH LEARNERS:
PAST, PRESENT, AND FUTURE

Traditional practices such as explicit teaching of grammatical structures and
direct instruction in listening, speaking, reading, and writing in order to

achieve communicative competence in English need to evolve to meet the needs of today's student. The 21st century English learner must become adept at the 5 C's (critical thinking, communication, collaboration, creativity, and culture) as well as master a new language while also attaining complex, grade-level academic content. This is no small feat! Therefore, teachers must find innovative ways to foster digital literacy and provide English learners with targeted, student-centered instruction. By modeling the appropriate use of technology and engaging English learners with the tools and strategies in this book, teachers will not only improve academic outcomes and enhance language acquisition but also cultivate digital citizenship.

DIGITAL AGE LEARNING EXPERIENCE

Let's start with an overview of current technology integration models and instructional strategies along with insight on the application of these resources to ELD/ESL instruction. The use of technology in the classroom is not the goal in and of itself. When a technology tool is successfully integrated into a classroom, the technology itself becomes "invisible" and supports teachers as they create, deliver, and assess learning experiences to engage students and improve academic outcomes in an exciting new way.

Before we can begin to explore the various ways that technology can enrich and even redefine instruction, let's review something that every teacher had to learn in college. Do you recall Bloom's taxonomy? Take a look at the 21st century version that has turned Bloom's taxonomy literally upside down (see Figure 1.1). The skills are inverted as students begin with creating, then move up the pyramid through evaluating, analyzing, applying, understanding, and finally, remembering. According to Shelley Wright (2012), "In the 21st century, we flip Bloom's Taxonomy. Rather than starting with knowledge, we start with creating and eventually discern the knowledge that we need from it." An important part of transforming education for ELs, and for all students in the digital age, is the shift in priority from students as consumers of information to students as creators.

This is good news for ELs, because the 21st century shift in Bloom's taxonomy as just described means increased opportunities for students to interact with peers and use English in context to complete authentic tasks. Bloom's 21 is a natural approach for ELD/ESL instructors who already understand the importance of using the four skills + 1 (listening, speaking, reading, writing, and viewing) to apply content and language knowledge in order to remember information. Carefully scaffolded questioning techniques lead ELs to evaluate and analyze tasks that require higher-order thinking skills and develop academic discourse.

Figure 1.1　Bloom's 21

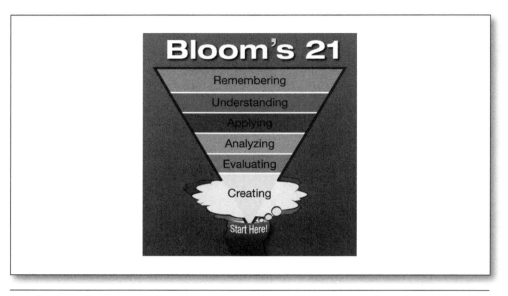

https://shelleywright.wordpress.com/2012/05/29/flipping-blooms-taxonomy.

Later in this book, we discuss the benefits of inverting the classroom for ELs through the flipped instructional model. The flipped methodology is neatly aligned to best practices for ELD/ESL instruction and includes an added dimension of using new technologies for direct instruction in order to provide more time for hands-on learning. With an understanding of Bloom's 21 and the flipped learning model, teachers of ELs invert the traditional classroom and build a foundation for self-directed learning.

ISTE STANDARDS

The ISTE Standards

Throughout this book we'll reference the International Society for Technology in Education Teacher and Student Standards. We have incorporated these standards in each chapter in order to provide guideposts for lesson planning and delivery. Here are the categories for each set of standards.

ISTE Standards for Teachers

1. Facilitate and inspire student learning and creativity

2. Design and develop digital age learning experiences and assessments

3. Model digital age work and learning

4. Promote and model digital citizenship and responsibility

5. Engage in professional growth and leadership

ISTE Standards for Students

1. Creativity and innovation

2. Communication and collaboration

3. Research and information fluency

4. Critical thinking, problem solving, and decision making

5. Digital citizenship

6. Technology operations and concepts

UNDERSTANDING ELs

The Understanding ELs section in each chapter offers specially selected methodologies and recommended strategies directly connected to the theme of the chapter. These research-informed strategies were chosen based on both seminal publications and current studies.

Who are our English learners? How can we best respond to the diversity among this student population? Honigsfeld and Dove (2015) suggest that educators recognize and carefully address the complex variation that exists among ELs. It has been noted that ELs are far from being a homogenous group requiring a one-size-fits-all approach; instead, they may differ based on the following factors: (a) immigration status, (b) prior schooling, (c) level of language proficiency in the native tongue or in any additional languages, (d) level of literacy in languages other than English, (e) level of language proficiency in English, and (f) the student's learning trajectory. See Table 1.1 and reflect on which of these groups and subgroups of ELs you work with in your own school.

The purpose of this summary table is to alert our readers to the vast *within-group* diversity that they are likely to encounter when working with ELs and to offer a quick reference guide to the complex background experiences and readiness levels that are to be expected among ELs. The technology tools and practices we suggest will also have to be carefully selected, adjusted, or modified to best match the needs of ELs. To better understand the unique background experiences and cultural knowledge that ELs bring to the school, educators must not only collaborate with each

Table 1.1 Diversity Among English Language Learners

Immigration status	❑ Recently arrived in the United States under typical circumstances ❑ Recently arrived in the United States as a refugee ❑ Recently arrived in the United States without legal documentation ❑ Temporarily living in the United States or visiting the United States ❑ U.S.-born, U.S. citizen
Prior education	❑ Formal, grade-appropriate education in another country ❑ Formal, grade-appropriate education in U.S. school system for a certain period of time ❑ Limited formal, grade-appropriate education in another country ❑ Interrupted formal, grade-appropriate education in another country ❑ Interrupted formal, grade-appropriate education in U.S. school system
Linguistic development in language(s) other than English	❑ Monolingual in native language only ❑ Bilingual in two languages other than English ❑ Bidialectal speaking both a standard language other than English and a dialect or Creole/Patois ❑ Multilingual in three or more languages
Status of language proficiency and literacy in language(s) other than English	❑ Only receptive language skills ❑ Productive oral language skills ❑ Limited literacy skills ❑ Grade-level literacy skills ❑ Any or all of the above skills in more than one language other than English
Level of English language proficiency	❑ *Emerging:* Being exposed to English with no or very limited language production ❑ *Beginning:* Demonstrating receptive and emerging productive language skills ❑ *Developing:* Employing basic oral and written language skills with predictable error patterns ❑ *Expanding:* Employing more advanced oral and written language skills with fewer errors ❑ *Transitioning:* Approximating native language proficiency
Learning trajectory	❑ Demonstrating typical academic and linguistic developmental trajectories ❑ Demonstrating academic and linguistic developmental challenges and difficulties that respond to interventions ❑ Demonstrating academic and linguistic developmental challenges and difficulties that require special attention

Adapted from Honigsfeld and Dove, 2015, p. 4.

other and engage in ongoing professional learning opportunities; they can also reach out to the community both physically and virtually. Creating multilingual, interactive online resources for parents of ELs that identify what they need to know about enrolling their child and supporting their learning in an American school is an often overlooked opportunity to enhance parent engagement.

When English learners represent such complex subgroups as depicted in Table 1.1, teachers may find it overwhelming to find out and keep in mind each student's background information regarding the following key questions:

- Were there any unusual circumstances such as trauma surrounding the child's arrival to the United States?
- Is there sufficient information available about the child's previous educational background, and how can the transition to the U.S. school system be as seamless as possible?
- What is the child's language proficiency and literacy level in the home language, in English, and in any additional languages?
- Are there any indications of gaps in education, learning difficulties, or other predictable challenges?

Table 1.2   ELL Profile-at-a-Glance Form

Name: _____   Date: _____

Student Background Information

Student Strengths	Student Needs

Academic Goals

Language Development Goals

Accommodations or Modifications (if necessary)

Adapted from Honigsfeld and Dove, 2015.

We suggest maintaining important information about the ELs in your school in a student management system or database for student profiles such as ones provided in Infinite Campus, Power School, or Ellevation that would allow each teacher to have access to basic information about each EL. Teachers can also create their own database by using Google Forms to survey their students individually using the profile template shown in Table 1.2.

MAKE-IT-YOUR-OWN LESSON SEEDS

In order to meet the academic needs of English learners, we have included sample lesson seeds that you can adapt to your own classroom. Each lesson seed includes learning targets, as well as sections for activating students' prior knowledge and promoting engagement and collaboration. The lesson seeds are intended to demonstrate how ELs can be supported through scaffolded instructional strategies along with technology tools. The checklist in each lesson seed is designed to highlight key elements that should be considered when planning instruction for ELs.

The lesson seeds are shared as a quick reference of ideas to help teachers in the deeper development of a comprehensive lesson plan. Teachers can add their own strategies and content when expanding the lesson seed.

Each lesson seed accomplishes the following:

1. **Sets student goals that encompass 21st century skills**
   Learning targets allow students to understand what they are expected to learn and how to demonstrate what they have learned. As mentioned earlier, 21st century lessons must integrate core content, with technology and language targets that relate to real-world communication and collaboration. ELs must be empowered to take ownership of their learning and effectively develop communicative skills through a variety of appropriate technologies.

2. **Activates students' prior knowledge**
   Activating prior knowledge helps ELs make connections to the new information they are learning in the classroom. Educators can tap into what students already know by first assessing prior knowledge and skills and then making connections between the new concepts being taught and the students' knowledge and experiences. ELs whose funds of knowledge are not aligned to what is taught in U.S. schools greatly benefit from activities that explicitly build foundational skills and background information.

3. **Enhances student engagement**
   Teachers can make content accessible for English learners by providing an environment in which students learn by doing. Teachers can differentiate

instruction through a blend of technology resources that provide a variety of modes of communication and entry points. ELs can then interact with the content and participate as active learners in the classroom. Educators need to deliver instruction in a manner that is comprehensible to students and meets the language demands of grade-level content. Including explicit instruction of academic language is important to the development of higher-order thinking processes associated with literacy and academic settings.

High levels of student engagement may be achieved through careful planning of learning activities that motivate students while also providing opportunities for frequent student-to-student interactions within the classroom. For ELs, activities should integrate all language skills (listening, speaking, reading, writing, and viewing), as well as address digital literacy and empower ELs to apply content and language knowledge using technology resources.

CONSIDER THIS

To support critical thinking about the chapter content and to allow for immediate application of new learning to your own context, we offer a reflection and thinking prompt in each chapter, called Consider This. It contains a question or a unique scenario, which may also offer an extension to the discussion in the chapter.

DIGITAL AGE EXPLORER'S CORNER

Creating Professional Learning Networks

In order to provide a vision for the digital age classroom, in this section we share vignettes from educators who are bravely exploring the digital age frontier by incorporating technology into their learning environments in creative ways. Our first digital age explorer has found a simple but effective way to bring teachers together to discuss classroom technology.

Great Neck Schools has promoted the formation of professional development groups (PDGs). PDGs are professional learning networks within each school in the district. Professional learning networks

(Continued)

(Continued)

(PLNs) are similar to collegial circles but also include an online component to help build capacity and foster collaboration among teachers. In order to support teachers as they work toward integrating technology into their classroom, Great Neck's professional development groups (PDGs) conduct peer-led informal gatherings that meet regularly for 30 minutes to discuss instructional technology. During each session, one person volunteers to demonstrate a particular technology application or lesson that he or she is currently using with students. This sharing of best practices and the peer discussion that ensues promotes professional growth and leadership within the learning organization.

PLN QUESTIONS

We encourage teachers to create professional learning networks within their own communities. To ensure a comprehensive approach, PLNs can be composed of content area, ELD/ESL, and technology specialists and should extend participation to a virtual space via online social networks such as Twitter, Facebook, Ning, Edmodo, or Google Classroom. #ELLchat is an example of a very popular online PLN.

To facilitate discussions about ELD/ESL methodology and technology integration, you will find targeted questions at the end of each chapter that encourage conversation based on the central themes and ideas presented.

1. What role do you think technology should play in educating English learners?

2. What types of technology do you currently use with ELs in your school and why?

3. How does Bloom's 21 pertain to the ELD/ESL classroom and the use of technology?

4. How can technology help to create a more student-centered learning environment?

5. How can the P21 framework guide instruction for ELs?

TOOLS AND RESOURCES

A complete list of technology resources is provided in Appendix A. ELD/ESL methodology resources are provided in Appendix B.

UNCOVERING THE CURRICULM FOR ELs

With the arrival of college and career readiness standards and even more rigorous standardized assessments, meeting the needs of linguistically and academically diverse learners is more challenging than ever before. Teachers dedicate time to "covering" curriculum that many ELs are not yet ready to learn because of language and sociolinguistic barriers. Rather than "cover" curriculum, this book is designed to help teachers "uncover" curriculum for ELs through the use of technology. As ELD/ESL instructors, we understand the complex demands all teachers face when working with ELs. We hope that this book will provide educators with ideas and everyday applications for using technology with ELs.

2 Fostering a Digital Learning Environment

Today's students will not live in a world where things change relatively slowly (as many of us did) but rather one in which things change extremely rapidly—daily and exponentially. So today's teachers need to be sure that, no matter what subjects they are teaching, they are teaching it with the future in mind. (Marc R. Prensky, 2010, p. 5)

OVERVIEW

In this chapter, teachers will learn how to "work" their classrooms by fostering an environment that provides opportunities for student communication, collaboration, creativity, and critical thinking. The digital learning environment allows for teachers to differentiate their instruction by creating a classroom space that supports content, language, and technology targets. The digital learning classroom offers a unique experience for each student that is centered on active learning and student engagement. Within this chapter, teachers will discover that creating a digital learning environment is not about using every digital tool or application available, it's about choosing the right one to enhance instruction and provide ELs equity and accessibility within the classroom. As teachers, we may not be able to control whether students have access to technology or Internet resources at home; however, providing access to a range of technology tools in the classroom is vital for ELs. ELs must use technology in a productive and collaborative classroom environment that will help develop language, literacy, and discipline-specific skills needed for college and career readiness. Teachers can share with ELs new technologies and resources that promote future educational and global opportunities.

For English learners, a digital learning environment provides opportunities to engage in the learning process and gain essential digital and informational literacy skills needed for real-life situations. Teachers move away from traditional direct instruction and become facilitators of a classroom where the delivery of instruction is based on personalized learning, inquiry and research, and positive student engagement. As Alan November (2012) stated, "while life outside of our schools has changed dramatically over the past century, we cling to an early industrialized classroom model that often fails to encourage collaboration, innovation, a global work ethic, or critical problem-solving skills. Our students are caught in a process we call "cover the curriculum," regardless of their mastery of the material." Within this chapter, we discuss the components of a digital age learning environment and classroom technology tools as they relate specifically to the instructional needs of English learners.

DIGITAL AGE LEARNING EXPERIENCE

Teacher Engagement

A digital learning environment requires that teachers enhance and support their instruction with innovative ways to use classroom technology tools. Within a digital learning environment, technology is an instructional tool and not the subject of instruction. It promotes and extends learning for English learners. To begin, teachers and administrators must be effective users of classroom technology tools. For many teachers, integrating technology can be overwhelming while they work toward meeting the routine demands of state learning standards, delivery of content, and formalized assessments. Eventually, teachers will recognize that creating a digital learning environment will support these efforts and encourage a shift in teaching from *what we learn* to *how we learn*.

Schools can support a culture of sharing and learning for all technology users. With this said, schools can promote the use of technology by training teachers and modeling the effective use of technology tools in their classrooms. Teachers can become active learners in the classroom along with their students and move away from the lecture-based setting by facilitating new student-driven models of instruction. The classroom can become a student-centered environment with an emphasis on meeting various learning styles and readiness that encourage ELs to gain understanding in their new language.

Today's current and developing technology tools have expanded opportunities for teachers to provide real-world experiences by virtualizing their classrooms. For example, podcasting platforms are the perfect tool to help English learners verbally share their ideas without the barrier of text. Podcasting platforms such as audioBoom or VoiceThread can easily open doors to global communication for ELs who may be limited in how much they can participate in the classroom. By podcasting, students can create web-based podcasts, share audio clips, or access audio content online. Students can show what they've learned by creating podcast tutorials to review concepts learned in the classroom.

Whether the teacher is a beginner or expert in using technology, finding the technology tools that meet the needs of ELs in the classroom can be a daunting task. Teachers can begin to examine ways to integrate technology and foster a digital age environment by taking a closer look at

1. differentiating the content of what they teach,

2. identifying how students will demonstrate what they have learned, and

3. redesigning the physical structure of the classroom environment.

Teachers become the "guide on the side" and welcome a more active classroom where students can work together and where teachers can provide continuous feedback, evaluation, and support.

ADVANTAGES FOR ELs

One significant advantage of a digital learning environment is that ELs will be motivated and encouraged to share their learning experiences regardless of their language proficiency and prior knowledge, which can oftentimes limit their academic success in the classroom. Strive to provide a safe school environment where ELs of all proficiency levels can interact with their classmates to improve academic content knowledge and language skills using traditional communication methods along with technology tools. Do not segregate ELs by proficiency level for all learning activities; instead use flexible grouping strategies that allow for different levels of ELs to interact with each other and their English-speaking peers for some of the time, whereas at other times they may be grouped homogeneously, especially when foundational skills are addressed. Whenever possible, the students who are proficient and literate in their home languages should have the opportunity to use their native language skills to build comprehension of the target content and to improve communication in their new language as well. Furthermore, a truly welcoming, inclusive school building will recognize students' home languages as assets and as cultural and linguistic bridges and not consider them as something students need to give up and replace with English.

Contrary to the traditional classroom where teachers spend most of their day standing in front of students teaching content, the digital learning environment builds on students' interaction in a structured approach, through problem solving, inquiry, and research. Teachers model and demonstrate learning by conducting mini-lessons to build background knowledge, preteach vocabulary, scaffold instruction, and model effective ways to use classroom technology tools. Teachers can address the needs of ELs and provide direct instruction to groups or individuals of all language proficiency levels. Students then use classroom technology tools while working in groups, pairs, or independently in a learning space that supports movement and discussion among all learners. When students are able to have a voice in the classroom in this fashion, we enable them to self-direct their own learning process.

THE CLASSROOM SETTING

The structure, design, and physical space within the classroom allow for students to work with peers and encourage investigative learning. "Learning happens anywhere and can be synchronous or asynchronous, formal or informal. The change from passive to active learning and the tensions created in this process affect teaching and learning strategies, technologies and space" (Steelcase, 2014, p. 4). The typical classroom is designed to provide student learning in a traditional direct-instruction environment, whereas the digital learning classroom supports multiple teaching approaches and access to individualized learning and peer-to-peer engagement. In a digital learning classroom, the physical space is set up to allow for movement among students as they actively work within the classrooms in pairs or groups and use technology as a tool for learning. What is the role of a teacher in such a scenario? Teachers must move away from a passive learning environment to an active learning environment. Teachers no longer need to stand in the front of the classroom controlling the learning process. Instead, teachers can take the time to use technology to collaborate with students and personalize instruction to help groups or individual students through the learning process. You can begin to create a digital learning environment by exploring the effects of technology integration on your classroom, including its physical structure. Does your classroom provide a collaborative and language-enriched environment for ELs?

USING CLASSROOM TECHNOLOGY TOOLS

When supporting the unique learning styles of ELs, there are certain features to consider when using current and emerging technology tools in the classroom:

- *Tools that encourage collaboration between the teacher and students (for example, productivity tools).* Productivity tools streamline the classroom workflow and can support ELs with note taking, word comprehension, and organizational skills that can help drive academic success.
- *Tools that allow teachers to manage lessons, create and share content, and connect with other colleagues (for example, social learning platforms).* Social learning platforms or learning management systems allow teachers to easily manage their classrooms. The platform allows for class discussions, assignments, and student collaboration within a learning community.
- *Tools that give students options to show off their knowledge (such as, screencasts or multimedia presentations).* Multimedia tools allow teachers to create presentations to increase student learning. Students can create multimedia presentations by using text, audio, images, and video to tell digital stories and create interactive video presentations.

Digital learning environments support the International Society for Technology in Education Standards for Teachers ISTE 2. a–d:

2. Design and Develop Digital Age Learning Experiences and Assessments

   Teachers design, develop, and evaluate authentic learning experiences and assessments incorporating contemporary tools and resources to maximize content learning in context and to develop the knowledge, skills, and attitudes identified in the ISTE Student Standards.

   a. Design or adapt relevant learning experiences that incorporate digital tools and resources to promote student learning and creativity.

   b. Develop technology-enriched learning environments that enable all students to pursue their individual curiosities and become active participants in setting their own educational goals, managing their own learning, and assessing their own progress.

   c. Customize and personalize learning activities to address students' diverse learning styles, working strategies, and abilities using digital tools and resources.

   d. Provide students with multiple and varied formative and summative assessments aligned with content and technology standards, and use resulting data to inform learning and teaching.

SOURCE: International Society for Technology in Education (2016).

- *Tools that develop language skills through listening, speaking, reading, writing, and viewing (such as podcasts, blogs, e-book readers).* ELs can develop language skills by using mobile devices to readily access e-books and online blogs to build comprehension and higher-order thinking skills.
- *Tools that allow teachers and students to collect, share, and organize resources (for example, QR codes, file hosting services).* Classroom information can be quickly accessed and shared remotely and allow for more interaction among teachers, students, and parents.

UNDERSTANDING ELs

Fostering Receptive and Productive Language Skills Through Student Engagement

Dove, Honigsfeld, and Cohan (2014) emphasize the need for inquiry-based, highly participatory, and engaging learning experiences for ELs and propose the following three critical considerations that benefit all learners:

- Replace lecturing and teacher-dominated, teacher-fronted classes with opportunities for student-directed discovery.
- Shift the classroom interaction from teacher talk to student discussion and extended student responses.
- Invite critical thinking and student ownership of learning through inquiry-based instruction.

ELs will only acquire language and content if they have access to the material, if it is presented through a variety of approaches and methodologies with ample support and scaffold (see mediating strategies to follow) so as to make the lesson comprehensible. Yet it is not enough for ELs to develop strong receptive skills; they need to actively and authentically use the language both in speaking and writing. Allowing for digital storytelling with tools such as Storybird or creating an interactive webpage with Weebly supports and scaffolds instruction via all five language skills.

Mediating Language and Content Through Instructional, Linguistic, Graphic, Visual, and Interactive Supports

Instructional Support

Instructional support can be successfully offered through the gradual release of responsibility model (Fisher & Frey, 2008; Pearson & Gallagher,

1983). This framework of instruction starts out with teacher modeling and moves on to delivering instruction to enhance student understanding in small groups and gradually increasing student independence as the lesson progresses. The four steps are the following:

1. Focus lesson: The teacher sets a purpose for the lesson and models a skill, strategy, or learning task for all learners.

2. Guided instruction: Students practice the new skills alongside the teacher, who differentiates instruction based on students' needs.

3. Student collaboration: Students work in productive learning groups as they engage in a variety of meaningful activities that allow them to interact, solve problems, and gain a clearer understanding of the lesson.

4. Independent practice: Students apply what they have learned.

Classroom instruction that is scaffolded this way allows for various well-supported, structured occasions for students to learn and practice new content and language.

Linguistic Support

Most frequently, teachers provide linguistic support by defining key vocabulary; preteaching essential words and phrases needed for the lesson; and using sentence frames, sentence starters, or paragraph frames to encourage student participation and enhance language production. Apps such as Wordle and Word Mover can be fun and creative ways to explore essential words and phrases. Using the native language will also offer linguistic support to ELs, as will teachers' conscious efforts to adjust their own speech and other text-based resources. Many translation apps and online resources can assist educators in this endeavor. Word cloud generators, such as Wordle, facilitate the study of key words for ELs (see Figure 2.1).

Visual Support

ELs exponentially benefit from seeing what they are also hearing. When visuals are available to supplement verbal input, the additional information gained from the images not only aids in comprehension but helps frontload the instruction by activating students' prior knowledge or building background knowledge much needed for the forthcoming lesson. Visual support can be created by using models, manipulatives, or realia;

Figure 2.1 Wordle Example

wordle.net

traditional images such as photographs, drawings, or sketches; or digital tools that incorporate video clips, clipart, Google Images, or websites such as BrainPOP ESL.

Graphic Support

Similar to the visual support just presented, graphic representations of complex concepts, difficult content, new skills, or language input can also contribute to better understanding and easier processing of the lesson. These tools aid in planning and organizing students' own thoughts as they prepare to speak or write about the new content, thus supporting both oral language production and written work. Holt Interactive Graphic Organizers (https://my.hrw.com/nsmedia/intgos/html/igo.htm) offer a wide variety of frequently used graphic supports, including a range of graphic organizers, charts, tables, timelines, and outlines.

Interactive Support

Finally, support may be provided to ELs through a variety of interactive structures. Whole-class or large-group lessons must be frequently interspersed or supplemented with pair work, triad, or other small-group activities. When students *stop and process* or *turn and talk* about the topic, time is allotted for them to formulate their own ideas and practice using academic language. In many classrooms, rotation stations, learning centers, or learning stations are frequently used approaches to group work, in which students collaboratively solve a problem, complete a task, and take ownership of new learning and the academic language and literacy skills connected to them.

MAKE IT YOUR OWN

The survey in Table 2.1 can help teachers identify the technology they are currently using and why, their comfort level with using technology, and how that technology is employed in the physical classroom space. By completing the survey, teacher leaders can recognize professional development needs and assist teachers in the technology planning process.

Table 2.1 Technology Survey

1. How confident are you when using technology in your classroom?
2. What challenges do you face when managing technology in your classroom?
3. What support do you need to effectively integrate technology in your classroom?
4. Does your classroom setting promote interactive group work among students?
5. Does the configuration of the desks or tables allow you to interact freely with groups?
6. Which technology tools do you use in your classroom for teaching and learning?
7. What are the key skills your students will develop by using technology?

CONSIDER THIS

The presence of technology does not make a digital learning environment. Consider what does: a classroom, school, and home environment for ELs that supports full interaction of technology and serves as a scaffolding tool for language and literacy development as well as a learning tool for content attainment. Figure 2.2 is an example of a learning space that encourages an interactive language-enriched environment.

Figure 2.2 Steelcase Node Active Classroom

Steelcase.com

DIGITAL AGE EXPLORER'S CORNER

Personalized Learning Solutions

Many school districts are transforming the learning environment by implementing a one-to-one iPad initiative. During a tour of a middle school, students shared their learning experiences using the iPad and eSpark, a personalized learning solution for the iPad. Students were able to explain how eSpark creates a playlist of educational apps and activities on their iPad by identifying their learning needs based on reading and math assessment data. For example, if a student demonstrates weakness in reading comprehension, eSpark provides apps and activities to help that student remediate that weakness. Teachers monitor academic progress on eSpark and use the data to inform instruction in the classroom. Students were enthusiastic and eager to show us what they've learned and were able to describe the goals and objectives of the program with great clarity and understanding.

This one-to-one iPad initiative has changed the physical space and environment for the students. By carefully arranging the classrooms, this school has managed to set up work areas that are conducive to individual and group learning. The classroom environment promotes engagement by allowing students to move easily inside and outside of the classroom in order to access different areas for information and materials. This school has intentionally developed a climate and culture to encourage deeper engagement among students, which is reflected by the physical environment.

CHAPTER SUMMARY

A digital learning environment is based on personalized learning, inquiry and research, and positive student engagement.

Teachers become the "guide on the side," providing continuous feedback, evaluation, and support.

The digital learning environment will encourage a shift in teaching from what we learn to how we learn.

Teachers meet the needs of ELs by providing direct instruction to groups or individuals of all language proficiency levels.

Students use classroom technology tools while working in groups, pairs, or independently in an active learning environment.

The structure, design, and physical space of the classroom allow for students to work with peers and encourage investigative learning.

The digital learning classroom supports multiple teaching approaches and access to individualized learning and peer-to-peer engagement.

Physical space is set up to allow for movement among students as they actively work within the classrooms using technology as a tool for learning.

The teacher is not restricted to the front of the classroom but can flow freely among the students to provide additional support.

Teachers choose classroom technology tools that support the instructional needs of ELs.

PLN QUESTIONS

1. How can a digital learning environment be used to meet the needs of English learners?

2. Reflect on a time when you changed your teaching style or lesson to meet the needs of your students. What prompted you to do so? What resources did you change, and what was the result?

3. What steps can you take to move from a teacher-centered environment to a student-centered environment?

4. Describe how you can integrate classroom technology tools in your current teaching practice.

5. Does the structure and physical space of your classroom encourage collaboration among students?

3 The Four Skills + 1 (Listening, Speaking, Reading, Writing, and Viewing)

Make no mistake about it: using popular culture, mass media, and digital media motivates and engages students. And students need to be motivated and engaged—genuine learning simply doesn't happen without it. (Renee Hobbs, 2011, p. 6)

OVERVIEW

In this chapter, we explain how using digital media in the classroom can allow ELs to access academic content in a whole new way by removing boundaries and promoting the language skills of listening, speaking, reading, writing, and viewing. The benefits of using digital media resources such as images and video streaming provide ELs a multisensory experience while introducing new concepts and ideas. Presenting content in multiple ways helps ELs to retain information and addresses the need to reinforce vocabulary development, comprehension, and background knowledge. This approach can be helpful for "ever ELs" (students who have been identified as English learners at any point during their enrollment in the school system) or former limited English proficient students (FLEPs) who typically no longer receive targeted services, although it is well documented that these students' language acquisition and literacy development may not have reached native-like proficiency. Hattie and Yates (2014) suggest that learning is a deliberate process—slow in pace; it does not often occur without sufficient time, focus, support, monitoring, and practice: "Impressions of quick learning are deceptive for many reasons. Unless the material is strongly meaningful, relevant and timely, it is subject to rapid and substantial forgetting. . . . To become skilled in a new area takes about 50 to 100 hours of practice" (p. 113).

Digital media is clearly an instructional method that generates a much greater amount of interest and engagement than more traditional reading matter and provides the repetition and reinforcement that ELs need to gain academic language proficiency. Digital media can offer the much-needed continued engagement with language that will yield higher levels of competence in English for ever ELs or FLEPs.

DIGITAL AGE LEARNING EXPERIENCE

English learners develop basic communication skills during day-to-day interactions with peers and teachers, but how do we help our English learners develop the cognitive communicative skills needed to be successful in academic settings? The linguistic and contextual structure of vocabulary used in a school setting (for example, a social studies text versus a science text) challenges ELs as they learn academic content. In addition, ELs encounter difficulties when attempting to communicate ideas and concepts because of their unfamiliarity of the grammatical arrangement of the words in phrases and sentences used in academic discourse. Digital media presentations should be used often to support language learning within the classroom.

The use of digital media also provides a low-anxiety environment with a focus on the traditional four language skills (listening, speaking, reading, writing), plus the skill of viewing, which must be included in today's classroom. ELs need ample production opportunities to develop language skills. When students experience language development through digital media, they begin to listen for understanding, speak to communicate ideas, and comprehend what they read in order to express their learning through their writing. Digital media provides ELs the ability to view and make connections to spoken and written language.

ePals is a global community that connects educators from around the world. This is one example of digital age pen pals that incorporates media galleries and project-based learning. Teachers can search for learning partners based on country, age group, language, subject, keywords, and interests. Websites such as ePals offer an accessible platform to collaborate across the globe while developing listening, speaking, reading, writing, and viewing skills for ELs.

The six language arts, as designated by the National Council of Teachers of English (NCTE) and the International Literacy Association (ILA) (National Council of Teachers of English, 1996), are listening, speaking, reading, writing, viewing, and visually representing. The first four have traditionally been considered to be the language arts; however, because visual media has become more important in everyday life, viewing and visually representing have become more important as means of communicating (Roe & Ross, 2006). In this chapter we have discussed how viewing supports ELs as they make connections between prior knowledge and new information. ELs can then comprehend language by listening, speaking, reading, writing, and viewing in English. For ELs, using visual media from a variety of online sources supports the development of receptive and expressive skills. In the next chapter, we elaborate on how visually representing reinforces language acquisition for ELs. As shown in Table 3.1, digital media supports the language development of receptive and expressive skills as a means of communicating for ELs.

Table 3.1 Using Digital Media With ELs

Using Digital Media for Receptive Skills
Listening. Digital media offers English learners the opportunity to listen to authentic language with the ability to control the rate and to pause and repeat the listening activity. ELs can use digital audio and video recordings to sample real and authentic language.
Reading. English learners can use electronic texts and e-books to take in, interpret, and relate information to their own personal experiences. Online digital resources such as Newsela provide information to ELs at a reading level that's right for them.
Viewing. Viewing requires skills similar to reading comprehension skills for ELs. Viewing can include everything from images to video presentations. Instructional videos and resources such as Discovery Education and LearnZillion provide different modalities for ELs to gain understanding of concepts.
Using Digital Media for Expressive Skills
Speaking. English learners can orally communicate thoughts and ideas clearly and effectively using various forms of digital media. Students can narrate digital stories by making use of digital media tools like Kaizena or use Prezi to create a multimedia presentation to demonstrate understanding of the language.
Writing. Communication through print allows ELs to use digital media resources in everyday writing tasks. Through the use of class websites, blogs, and social networking, students can practice writing skills in a more supportive and low-anxiety environment. Blogging platforms such as Edublogs or WordPress or tools like Google Docs facilitate writing and collaboration.

The four skills + 1 support the International Society for Technology in Education Standards for Teachers ISTE 1. a–d:

1. Facilitate and Inspire Student Learning and Creativity

   Teachers use their knowledge of subject matter, teaching and learning, and technology to facilitate experiences that advance student learning, creativity, and innovation in both face-to-face and virtual environments.

   a. Promote, support, and model creative and innovative thinking and inventiveness.

   b. Engage students in exploring real-world issues and solving authentic problems using digital tools and resources.

   c. Promote student reflection using collaborative tools to reveal and clarify students' conceptual understanding and thinking, planning, and creative processes.

   d. Model collaborative knowledge construction by engaging in learning with students, colleagues, and others in face-to-face and virtual environments.

SOURCE: International Society for Technology in Education (2016).

Digital media offers many possibilities when working with ELs. The use of multiple modalities through visual and video support can provide teachers with scaffolding resources that foster different types of instructional practices. Teachers can provide learning experiences to students that ordinarily would not be available in the classroom. In organizing the many types of instructional practices, Renee Hobbs (2011) outlines the essential dimensions of digital and media literacy:

1. ACCESS. Finding and sharing appropriate and relevant information and using media texts and technology tools well.

2. ANALYZE. Using critical thinking to analyze message purpose, target audience, quality, veracity, credibility, point of view, and potential effects or consequences of messages.

3. CREATE. Composing or generating content using creativity and confidence in self-expression, with awareness of purpose, audience, and composition techniques.

4. REFLECT. Considering the impact of media messages and technology tools upon our thinking and actions in daily life and applying social responsibility and ethical principles to our own identity, communication behavior, and conduct.

5. ACT. Working individually and collaboratively to share knowledge and solve problems in the family, the workplace, and the community, and participating as a member of a community at local, regional, national, and international levels. (p. 12)

UNDERSTANDING ELs

The gateway to academic content is academic language. As Schleppegrell (2012) observed, "Academic language is functional for getting things done at school, varying as it is used in different subject areas and for different purposes, but requiring that children use language in new ways to learn and to display knowledge about what they have learned in ways that will be valued" (p. 410). Academic language is frequently conceptualized as having three levels: a word level, a sentence level, and a text level. These levels are not to be seen as isolated learning targets; rather, they are reminders of the important features of English that ELs need exposure to and ample opportunity to master. See Table 3.2 for a summary of these three academic language dimensions' distinct features, challenges ELs face as they work on mastering them, and key instructional practices for classroom use.

Using complex academic language in and outside the classroom goes beyond teaching words, practicing sentence structures, and reading increasingly complex texts. It involves students' learning to process and internalize new skills and information while also engaging in emerging

Table 3.2 Academic Language Dimensions, Features, Challenges, and Essential Instructional Practices

Dimension	Academic Language Features	Challenges for ELs	Essential Instructional Practices
Word level (vocabulary or phrases)	Generic and discipline-specific academic terms Figurative and idiomatic expressions Words with multiple meanings Roots and affixes	Volume of vocabulary needed Nuances of word meanings Phrases and collocations	Exposure to vast vocabulary through interactions with language-rich texts An interactive environment in which verbal exchanges are encouraged and not silenced Word learning strategies
Sentence level	Sentence structure Sentence length Grammatical structures Pronouns Context clues Proverbs	Complex sentences with low-frequency words Advanced grammatical features (passive voice, participles)	Sentence dissection (sentence chunking with discussion on the form and meaning of each segment) Scaffolded sentence frames Mentor text

(Continued)

Table 3.2 (Continued)

Dimension	Academic Language Features	Challenges for ELs	Essential Instructional Practices
Text level	Text organization Text craft and structure Text density Clarity and coherence Text types and genres	Reading and Lexile levels Complexity of ideas Background knowledge students need to comprehend Styles and structures unique to each genre or text type	Strategy instruction across the content areas Genre study Read-alouds and shared reading Scaffolded independent reading Inquiry groups Text analysis Text annotation

Adapted from O'Hara, S., Zwiers, J., & Pritchard, R. (2013). *Framing the development of complex language and literacy.* Retrieved from http://aldnetwork.org/sites/default/files/pictures/aldn_brief_2013.pdf

language use to communicate. For language to develop in a systemic way, ELs must be listening, speaking, reading, writing, and viewing authentically in their new language every day. Researchers and practitioners whose work is informed by sociocultural theory also believe that language acquisition and literacy learning happen when "knowledge and understanding are co-constructed through interaction, and through the practice of scaffolding, whereby the learner's understandings and attempts to express these in words are supported and assisted through dialogue" (Cullen, Kullman, & Wild, 2013, p. 426).

Consider the following listening and speaking strategies to encourage a more complex academic dialogue for ELs:

- Employ scaffolded "talk moves." Give your students appropriate sentence stems for various common language functions. Help them learn to ask for clarification when they do not understand something (Would you explain what _____ means?); paraphrase someone else's idea (What I heard you say is _____); extend what a classmate said (In addition to what ____ said,); or agree or disagree with others (I agree with _____ /I respectfully disagree with _____).
- Provide productive wait time that includes a quick write or quick draw. Students gather their thoughts, jot down some ideas, and enter the academic conversation feeling better prepared.

- Elicit longer answers from ELs who are at a more advanced language proficiency level. Invite students to elaborate on their short answers by encouraging them to give some examples, add more details, describe a person or object they mentioned, or explain their thinking further.
- Use flexible grouping configurations that include whole-group discussion sessions typically led by the teacher, small-group interactions, cooperative learning groups, triads, and pairs.

Some key research-based reading strategies that support ELs include the following:

- Conduct frequent formative assessments of ELs' reading development, such as how well they demonstrate letter-sound correspondence; letter recognition; word-, sentence-, and text-level reading comprehension; and fluency. Based on data, support ELs in the areas most needed and monitor their progress over time.
- Focus on Tier One and Tier Two vocabulary to address the meaning of everyday conversational phrases, idioms, and expressions that may cause confusion, as well as high-frequency, Tier Three academic words.
- Ask carefully constructed questions before, during, and after reading to support ELs' reading comprehension. Ask for literal responses that require students to recall factual information or readily available details. Probe them to offer their interpretations of what was read as well as engage in critical reflection, analysis, and application of the new information read.
- Read aloud to students and model comprehension strategies you use through thinking aloud or comprehending aloud (Zwiers, 2008). Allow students to gain insight into your reading comprehension process. When they hear what you did when you came across a certain word, how you interpreted the actions of a certain character, or how you made sense of a new piece of information in a nonfiction selection, they will see these examples as models of literacy actions they can emulate.

For ELs to develop writing skills, we need to make writing a daily occurrence. Dorfman and Cappelli (2007) also advocate for the study of exemplary written work such as mentor texts through which ELs can better understand what constitutes accomplished writing. Wolsey, Lapp, and Fisher (2010) claim that "all students are to act and believe that literacy is valued and valuable" (p. 10). Students can only achieve this goal if they experience the collective sense of importance literacy holds for the entire school community. When teachers collaborate to plan academic language learning and literacy development activities that meaningfully connect with each other, ELs can make better sense of the patterns in language and literacy.

Some key writing strategies we suggest include the following:

- Invite recently arrived ELs with high levels of literacy skills in their home language to write in that language. They can add illustrations or English-language labels that support their writing. As English proficiency grows, ask them to prepare a glossary of key ideas, an outline or bulleted list, or a brief summary in English.
- Provide writing scaffolds such as word boxes, sentence stems, paragraph frames, or essay outlines as needed.
- Use bilingual peer bridges, teaching assistants, and print and electronic resources such as bilingual glossaries and dictionaries to connect literacy in the home language with that of the new language.
- Introduce and maintain a variety of daily writing tasks that will activate students' prior knowledge and engage ELs in brief forms of response writing in response to a topic or text.
- Adapt the writing process to the needs of ELs by spending more time on prewriting, drafting, and editing; structuring writing tasks into shorter, more manageable subtasks; and guiding students through each step with questions and prompts, step-by-step directions, and modeling, as well as samples and exemplars.
- Support writing with visuals, diagrams, word banks, glossaries, lists of words, outlines, or templates as needed.

MAKE-IT-YOUR-OWN LESSON SEEDS

The following brief overviews provide a topic with "seed" ideas that we invite you to "grow" into a full lesson plan for your classroom.

The Life Cycle of a Butterfly

In the following lesson seed, students will learn how to observe, recognize, and describe the life cycle of a butterfly. Students will create storyboards to identify the parts of a caterpillar and butterfly. Students will then work with partners to observe and record the four stages of the life cycle of a butterfly and create a multimedia presentation.

The Life Cycle of a Butterfly

Grade Level: 1

Planning	Student Goals
Subject Area(s)	• **I can** make observations and identify the four stages of a butterfly's life cycle.

Planning	Student Goals

Student Goals

- **I can** make observations and identify the four stages of a butterfly's life cycle.
- **I can** record my observations and define the word *metamorphosis*.
- **I can** collaborate and create a multimedia presentation with my classmates using the ScreenChomp app.

Planning

Subject Area(s)

X	English language arts
	Mathematics
X	Science
	Social studies
	Other:

Language Skills

X	Listening
X	Speaking
X	Reading
X	Writing
X	Viewing

Resources and Supports

X	Technology tools
X	Native language
X	Visuals, realia, manipulatives
X	Graphic organizers

Interaction-Grouping

	Individual practice
	Pairs
X	Small group
	Whole group
	Online collaboration

Activating Prior Knowledge

Complete a K-W-L chart on what you know about butterflies.

View a brief video that illustrates the four stages of a butterfly's life cycle.

Listen to Eric Carle's story *The Very Hungry Caterpillar*.

Identify the four stages of a butterfly's life cycle.

Engagement

- Work in small groups to create storyboards of the life cycle of a butterfly.
- Create a ScreenChomp presentation using the group storyboards that incorporate audio, visuals, and text to demonstrate what you've learned.
- Use the ScreenChomp drawing tools to label, analyze, and annotate your whiteboard presentation.
- Present to the class your recorded ScreenChomp presentation.

Template adapted from WIDA Lesson Plan Share Space
https://www.wida.us/professionaldev/educatorresources/lessonPlan-shareSpace.aspx

(Continued)

(Continued)

Spend. Save. Donate.

This lesson seed is based on free resources from the National Endowment for Financial Education's (NEFE) High School Financial Planning Program (HSFPP). Teachers can request a free complete curriculum that includes videos, student guides, lesson plans, and other resources by visiting http://www.hsfpp.org and http://bizkids.com.

Spend. Save. Donate.		
Grade Level: 7		
Planning		**Student Goals**
Subject Area(s)		• **I can** develop a saving and spending plan for a weekend vacation.
X	English language arts	
X	Mathematics	• **I can** use financial terms and identify different types of expenses.
	Science	• **I can** use Microsoft Excel to create a budget spreadsheet and Prezi to present my vacation plan to the class.
X	Social studies	
X	Other: Financial literacy	
Language Skills		**Activating Prior Knowledge**
X	Listening	View "Spending and Planning" video from the hsfpp.org curriculum kit.
X	Speaking	Have you ever saved your money for something special? Did you create a plan?
X	Reading	What does the word *budget* mean to you?
X	Writing	Budgeting helps you know your income and expenses. You must know how much money you have before you can decide what you can afford to buy. A budget is a tool to help you meet your financial goals.
X	Viewing	
Resources and Supports		
X	Technology tools	
X	Native language	
X	Visuals, realia, manipulatives	**Engagement**
X	Graphic organizers	1. In pairs, plan for a weekend vacation. Research and decide on the following:
Interaction-Grouping		How much money will you need for transportation? (Include items such as gas, parking fees, bus fare, train tickets, airplane tickets.)
	Individual practice	
X	Pairs	Where will you eat? What will it cost?
	Small group	How much money will you need for groceries or food?
	Whole group	Where will you sleep, and how much will it cost?
	Online collaboration	

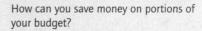

	How can you save money on portions of your budget?
	How will you save for your trip?
	2. Use Microsoft Excel to create a budget spreadsheet that itemizes and calculates the estimated expenses for the vacation.
	3. Using Prezi, create a presentation of your vacation plan that includes text and images.

Template adapted from WIDA Lesson Plan Share Space

https://www.wida.us/professionaldev/educatorresources/lessonPlan-shareSpace.aspx

CONSIDER THIS

A SWIRL-ing classroom is one in which students speak, write, interact, read, and listen authentically while constructing new knowledge, practicing emerging skills, and making meaning collaboratively. How does technology contribute to making SWIRL a 21st century goal for every classroom?

DIGITAL AGE EXPLORER'S CORNER

Multimedia "All About Me" E-Book

Jennifer Anderson, an ELD/ESL teacher from Stokes Elementary School, participates in a professional development consortium that is dedicated to helping ELD/ESL teachers incorporate technology into instruction. Bonnie Foster, a professional developer specializing in educational technology, worked with Jennifer to create an e-book that uses iPads and the app Book Creator with her ELs to add a new twist to an "All About Me" project. Together the class created an interactive e-book titled *Our Future* that included written text, student artwork, images, video, and sound narration to talk about their personal histories and future goals. The class book revolved around two questions: "Who am I?" and "What do I want to become?" For Chapter 1, the students researched their life story by conducting oral interviews of family members using a set of six questions. They used

(Continued)

(Continued)

this information to write an entry for the e-book and included family photographs and symbols of their heritage. For Chapter 2, they visited Pebblego.com to research different occupations and draw connections between the text and their own career aspirations. The students then created an audio recording describing their future goals and embedded it alongside their essay. At the end of the book there is an About the Author section. This consists of a video biography of each student in the class.

CHAPTER SUMMARY

The 4 + 1 language skills are listening, speaking, reading, writing, and viewing.

Digital media supports receptive and expressive academic language skills for ELs.

Digital media can be used to develop receptive skills in listening, reading, and viewing.

Digital media can be used to develop expressive skills in speaking and writing.

Visual and video support can provide teachers with scaffolding resources that foster different types of instructional practices.

Renee Hobbs outlines the essential dimensions of digital and media literacy to include the five elements of access, analyze, create, reflect, and act.

PLN QUESTIONS

1. How can digital media support real and authentic language in the classroom?

2. Are you currently using online digital resources? If so, how?

3. How can you use instructional videos and resources to increase student collaboration?

4. In what ways can you provide a more supportive and low-anxiety environment for ELs to express and support their speaking and writing skills?

5. Describe how students can demonstrate what they have learned through digital media.

4 Responding and Creating

Now your job is not to dispense knowledge. It's to facilitate learning. No longer is the teacher the bottleneck between students and knowledge. Rather, the teacher architects the environment—in the classroom, on the tablet, online, everywhere. (Robin Britt qtd. in Rotella, 2013)

OVERVIEW

In this chapter we explore the use of multimedia tools to support the creation of digital content to help students develop their critical thinking, reasoning and language skills, and creative confidence. If we want to transform instruction rather than simply enhance lessons with technology, we need to encourage ELs to contribute by using multimedia tools to create content that demonstrates both their academic knowledge and their proficiency in English. Empowering students to create and publish multimedia resources such as videos, podcasts, and e-books helps them organize and communicate their ideas more clearly and effectively. The inclusion of images, audio, and video assets accelerates the language learning process by providing a multisensory experience for the learner. This type of classroom experience helps ELs to make the shift from being just critical consumers of information to creators of authentic digital media resources. This leap is essential if we want to transform learning experiences for our 21st century ELs.

DIGITAL AGE LEARNING EXPERIENCE

The SAMR Model

Before we can discuss the creation of multimedia content, it is important for teachers to become familiar with the SAMR (substitution, augmentation, modification, redefinition) model. The SAMR model facilitates the digital learning transformation and can help guide teachers when selecting technology to use with their students. When teachers first begin to use technology in their lessons, they often begin by substituting what they already do in class with a digital version of the same thing. Flash cards are a good example of this process. Teachers have used paper flash cards for generations. Nowadays, many teachers create digital flash cards as a substitution for a traditional instructional practice. Understanding the SAMR model will help teachers assess the depth at which technology has been integrated into the curriculum. Dr. Ruben Puentedura designed this model to guide educators through four levels of technology integration to demonstrate how instructional practices that integrate technology can evolve over time. The first two levels, substitution and augmentation, offer an

Figure 4.1 The SAMR Model for Technology Integration

The SAMR Model for Technology Integration

SAMR

I wonder what's in the ocean?

NO TECH

SUBSTITUTION
Tech acts as a direct tool substitute, with no functional change.

AUGMENTATION
Tech acts as a direct tool substitute, with functional improvement

MODIFICATION
Tech allows for significant task redesign

REDEFINITION
Tech allows for the creation of new tasks, previously inconceivable.

ENHANCEMENT   TRANSFORMATION

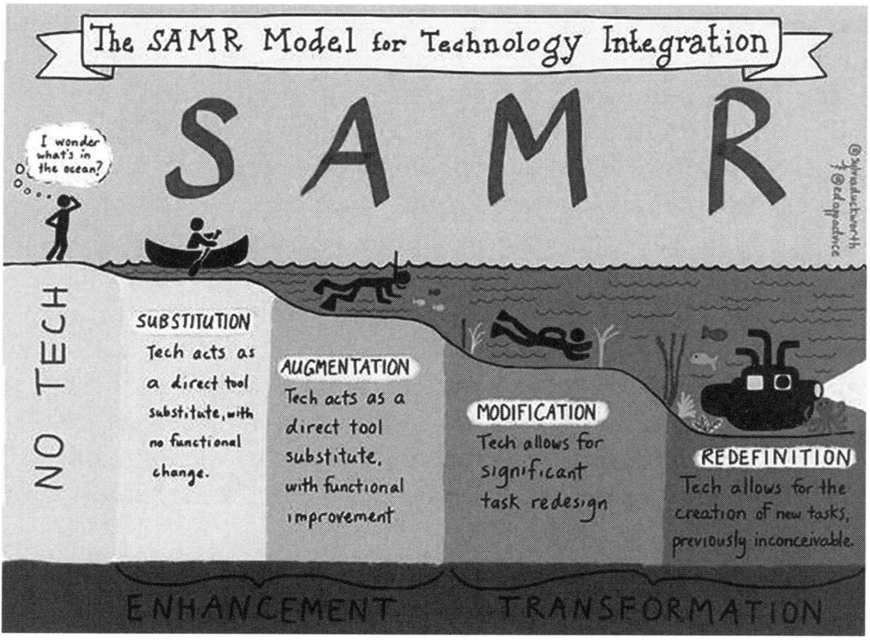

enhancement to previous practices, whereas the second two levels, modification and redefinition, provide deeper changes that transform traditional practices. Figure 4.1 illustrates how technology can be integrated into instructional tasks with increasing depth.

The four levels according to this model are described here.

1. *Substitution*. Technology acts as a direct tool substitute with no functional change. For example, a teacher who chooses to use flash cards to teach and reinforce vocabulary now has students create flash cards to learn vocabulary using apps such as Cramberry and Quizlet.

2. *Augmentation*. Technology acts as a direct tool substitute with functional improvement. For example, students create an e-book that incorporates audio and video to practice and learn vocabulary using an app such as Book Creator.

3. *Modification*. Technology allows for significant task redesign. Teachers reproduce or significantly modify the student task with social networking and collaboration. For example, students collaborate online to create and publish a blog that includes vocabulary definitions, video, and links to more information.

4. *Redefinition*. Technology allows for new tasks previously inconceivable. This allows students to interact and engage in learning in ways they could not do in the past and promotes deeper levels of study and research. It provides students with both a choice and personal voice in their learning and is based on problem solving that demonstrates originality of thought and creativity. For example, students from the United States use Skype to videoconference with students from China who are also learning English. Together they use the target vocabulary to collaborate on ways to solve a common problem that affects both communities of learners.

An awareness of the level of technology integration that a learning activity demands will inform the creation of more cognitively challenging tasks for students because as we move up the SAMR ladder, we also move up the inverted taxonomy of Blooms 21, described in Chapter 1 of this book.

The key to redesigning and redefining classroom tasks in order to reach transformative levels of technology integration is to tap into student creativity. Incorporating tools such as mobile devices and tablets provides opportunities for students to create and respond to lessons in new ways.

MOBILE DEVICES AND TABLETS FOR ELS

Multimedia Support for Content

Mobile devices and tablets not only enhance instruction and make academic content more accessible for English learners, but they have the potential to redefine traditional learning tasks. When the right educational mobile application is integrated into a content-rich lesson, it provides multisensory access to that content, facilitating comprehension and allowing ELs to participate more effectively in academic discourse. Apps can be used to scaffold activities that may otherwise be difficult for ELs to understand. In addition, using multimedia apps to deliver content enhances traditional methods of delivery that are largely text based. This opens the door to critical thinking by lowering the language barrier and channeling the instructional focus to academic content.

Multiple Modalities for Learning

Using iPads, Chromebooks, and other mobile devices for ELs is one way to provide scaffolding to students who are often faced with rigorous content demands while working on acquiring English proficiency at the same time. ELs need alternative pathways to access content.

According to Wilder (2010), the use and creation of multimodal texts will provide students with opportunities to use linguistic, visual, and audio modes in order to experience, conceptualize, analyze, and apply meaning.

Delivering content through tablets or similar mobile devices addresses multiple learning modalities, including visual, tactile, auditory, and kinesthetic learning preferences. It also provides an alternative way for students to demonstrate their content knowledge through the creation of digital media using a wide variety of apps.

Applications for 4 + 1 Language Skills

Mobile devices and tablets allow for the use of all language skills. The creation of dynamic, interactive e-books that incorporate video, sounds, links, interactive widgets, and high-quality images redefines writing and viewing assignments. ELs can develop active reading skills with the benefit of keyword searches, highlighting, defining, annotating, bookmarking, and researching at their fingertips. Using a text-to-speech feature allows English learners to hear the entire text or vocabulary word or phrase on demand. Listening, speaking, and viewing skills can be reinforced with the creation of teacher and student avatars, videos, and podcasts.

Several applications allow students and teachers to create remarkable user-friendly e-books that can be published on the web, printed, shared, or saved and stored locally. In a survey of AP and National Writing Project teachers, a majority said digital tools encourage students to be more invested in their writing by encouraging personal expression and providing a wider audience for their work. Most teachers also say digital tools make teaching writing easier (Purcell, Buchanan, & Friedrich, 2013).

Finally, iPads have many built-in accessibility settings that can be adjusted to help ELs access language more readily. This includes features such as text to speech, speech to text, rate of speech, and view settings: size of font, screen contrast, subtitles, and captioning. Enabling the guided access feature allows teachers to manage the iPad so that students can only work within one app or webpage. Apple Classroom allows teachers to manage groups and control the content that students can access while using iPads during instruction.

Informing Parents

When a new technology initiative such as the use of iPads, Chromebooks, or other mobile devices is deployed in your school, it is essential to keep parents informed throughout the implementation process. As needed, schools should offer translation services for parents of ELs at all technology orientation sessions. Here are some questions for parents to consider:

1. How will classwork expectations of my child change?

2. How will school expectations of me as a parent change?

3. What will a typical day in this new classroom environment look like?

4. What is the school's acceptable use policy (AUP)?

This instructional model aligns seamlessly with the International Society for Technology in Education Standards for Students ISTE 1. a–d.

1. Creativity and Innovation

   Students demonstrate creative thinking, construct knowledge, and develop innovative products and processes using technology.

   a. Apply existing knowledge to generate new ideas, products, or processes.

   b. Create original works as a means of personal or group expression.

   c. Use models and simulations to explore complex systems and issues.

   d. Identify trends and forecast possibilities.

SOURCE: International Society for Technology in Education (2016).

5. What training and development resources are being provided to the teachers?

6. What technology do I need to have at home in order for my child to complete assignments?

UNDERSTANDING ELs

Coplanning

One of the best ways to ensure that ELs will retain information and build academic language skills across the curriculum is to set aside time for coplanning with other teachers of ELs. Teacher collaboration is a critical component of ensuring curriculum continuity and providing instructional consistency. During specially designated coplanning times, general education and ESOL teachers may rely on each other's expertise, share resources, and accomplish the following:

- Establish content and language objectives and instructional procedures for reaching those objectives.
- Determine appropriate modifications and adaptations that will offer the necessary support to ELs.
- Plan differentiated, tiered learning activities that match ELs' proficiency levels and needs.
- Design formative assessment tools to be used to inform their instruction.
- Identify the most appropriate intervention strategies that will respond to the patterns of learning challenges students face.
- Discuss research-based best practices and promising strategies they wish to implement.

If ESOL and general-education teachers have the opportunity to codeliver instruction, each may focus on a different aspect of the lesson and experiment with a variety of coteaching models while also infusing technology to enhance content and language attainment (Honigsfeld & Dove, 2010, 2015).

Instructional Design Principles

One of the most important outcomes of the Understanding Language initiative at Stanford University (2013) has been the identification of six principles for designing appropriate instruction for ELs. Although these

Table 4.1 Six Principles for Designing Appropriate Instruction for ELs

Principle	Related Mobile Apps
1. Instruction focuses on providing ELs with opportunities to engage in discipline-specific practices that are designed to build conceptual understanding and language competence in tandem.	Butterfly HD Shakespeare in Bits Operation Math U.S. Geography
2. Instruction leverages ELs' home language(s), cultural assets, and prior knowledge.	Tabletop Translator Google Translate Dragon Dictation Speak It!
3. Standards-aligned instruction for ELs is rigorous and grade-level appropriate and provides deliberate and appropriate scaffolds.	Popplet Prezi FlockDraw iBooks Author
4. Instruction moves ELs forward by taking into account their English proficiency level(s) and prior schooling experiences.	Newsela Toontastic See.Touch.Learn Tellagami
5. Instruction fosters ELs' autonomy by equipping them with the strategies necessary to comprehend and use language in a variety of academic settings.	Evernote iStudiez EasyBib Notability
6. Diagnostic tools and formative assessment practices are employed to measure students' content knowledge, academic language competence, and participation in disciplinary practices. (Stanford University, January 2013, p. 1)	Quizlet Plickers Socrative Kahoot!

principles do not explicitly mention multimedia tools, the potential and promise of technology integration is clearly present. Table 4.1 summarizes the six principles and key mobile apps that are most closely aligned to each.

Literacy Development

Literacy skills are essential for ELs to develop so they can become successful both in and out of school. Among others, Goldenberg (2008) reports that ELs need explicit instruction similar to that of their English-speaking classmates, including phonemic awareness, phonics, vocabulary, comprehension, and writing. On the other hand, he suggests that teachers consider additional factors that lead to successful literacy learning such as "cooperative learning (students working interdependently on group instructional tasks and learning goals), encouraging reading in English, discussions to promote comprehension ('instructional conversations'), and mastery learning (which involves precise behavioral objectives permitting students to reach a 'mastery' criterion before moving to new learning)" (Goldenberg, 2008, p. 17). Instructional conversations can even be developed through group e-mails and text via mobile phone. Group e-mails and texting facilitate cooperative learning and reinforce language skills. While students cooperate they use their languages (both the target language and the home language) functionally. Using a mobile phone to participate in instructional conversations and other learning opportunities can be an essential tool for subgroups of ELs who may have limited access to technology due to a variety of circumstances. One such subgroup is migrant English learners.

Migrant English learners are children whose families typically work in the agricultural industries and as a result, will move from district to district or even from state to state several times within a 1- to 3-year time frame. Because the families follow the various seasonal crops, it is not unusual for their children to miss school if they also work in the fields alongside their parents. Migrant ELs are among the most transient student populations, so the most important strategy is to immediately familiarize them with the instructional routines and include them in class and school activities as much as possible. Enhance the appropriate grade-level or modified curriculum with multiple technology-based scaffolds to make the content accessible and personally engaging and meaningful. If migrant students have cell phones, the phones can be incorporated into instruction and provide meaningful connection to the classroom teacher and peers. Lundy-Ponce (2010) suggests "encouraging students to establish electronic mail 'pen-pal' relationships with migrant students when they leave the school so that a sense of continuity and the security of familiarity can be established" (Strategies for Success, para. 5).

It has also been established that during their academic career, students progress through four major literacy roles as they develop more and more advanced literacy skills (Fang, 2012): ELs, just like their English-speaking peers, must learn how to be code breakers, meaning makers, text users, and text analysts/critics, while also using digital tools in the process.

1. As code breakers, ELs begin by developing foundational literacy skills that provide the basis for decoding text written in English, whether presented in print or digital formats. There are many apps that support developing literacy skills. Bitsboard is one app that can be used to create customized activities to target emerging vocabulary and decoding skills.

2. As meaning makers, ELs begin to make sense of what the text means. First they are most likely to figure out the literal meaning of any text; however, with appropriate scaffolding and support, ELs can unlock further layers of meaning as well. Platforms such as Subtext and Actively Learn provide many interactive features that allow students and teachers to annotate and interact with digital text. Teachers can scaffold text by embedding videos and questions that aid comprehension for ELs.

3. As text users, ELs start to expand their reading skills and tackle a whole variety of texts. They not only comprehend what they read, they also become apt at responding to those texts. When ELs have opportunities to read high-interest texts, as well as make reading choices for themselves, their literacy lives become more authentic. An app that can develop a student's ability to respond to a variety of texts and develop independent reading skills is LightSail. LightSail is an e-reading app that allows for independent and guided reading. Students can make reading choices that are based on Lexile levels. It assesses and tracks a student's literacy development throughout the year and includes an interactive class discussion component.

4. As text analysts and critics, ELs take the next steps to independence and respond to what they read analytically and critically: they analyze, synthesize, and evaluate the readings while also participating in meaningful discussions with peers and their teachers. With the use of media tools, this type of interaction can reach beyond the classroom. One way to achieve this type of interaction is with online literature circles. Students can lead the circle by selecting a novel and creating their own substantive prompts. ReadWriteThink. org provides many suggestions for implementing online book discussions. For lesson plan ideas see "Thoughtful Threads: Sparking Rich Online Discussions" (http://www.readwritethink.org/class room-resources/lesson-plans/thoughtful-threads-sparking-rich-1165.html).

MAKE-IT-YOUR-OWN LESSON SEEDS

The following brief overviews provide a topic with "seed" ideas that we invite you to "grow" into a full lesson plan for your classroom.

Addition Word Problems

Solving word problems requires reading comprehension and mathematical skills. ELs have to learn how to read effectively to determine meaning, in addition to the mathematical processes needed to solve the word problem. In the following lesson seed, students will explore word problems and create their own. Students will work as a whole class and in small groups to analyze and construct their equations and communicate their results.

Addition Word Problems		
Grade Level: 2		

Planning		Student Goals
Subject Area(s)		• **I can** identify and analyze vocabulary that describes addition word problems.
X	English language arts	• **I can** listen to word problems and use drawings to orally represent the equation.
X	Mathematics	• **I can** collaborate with my teacher and classmates by using an interactive whiteboard to learn more advanced concepts.
	Science	
	Social studies	
	Other:	
Language Skills		**Activating Prior Knowledge**
X	Listening	Work together to solve addition problems. Use the content-specific math vocabulary words and make your own addition stories using the new vocabulary. Solve addition problems using illustrations to orally explain the equation on the interactive board.
X	Speaking	
X	Reading	
X	Writing	
X	Viewing	
Resources and Supports		**Engagement**
X	Technology tools	• Listen to the teacher tell addition stories to the whole class.
X	Native language	• Use drawings to represent the addition problem and retell the addition story to your partners.
X	Visuals, realia, manipulatives	• Write a number sentence (for example, $9 + 7 = 16$) to represent the addition story.
X	Graphic organizers	

Interaction-Grouping		Write an original addition story with your group using the Notebook software. Present your addition story to the class on the interactive whiteboard. Record yourself by using a Voki (mini avatar) to read the addition word problem to the class.
	Individual practice	
	Pairs	
X	Small group	
X	Whole group	● Share your addition word problem story on the class virtual wall (Padlet) for a peer review.
	Online collaboration	

Template adapted from WIDA Lesson Plan Share Space

https://www.wida.us/professionaldev/educatorresources/lessonPlan-shareSpace.aspx

Creating a Public Service Announcement About Drug Addiction

In this lesson students will conduct research on the topic of drug addiction. The teacher will use QR codes to curate appropriate resources for the students to use. Using the iMovie app, students will create a public service announcement to educate others about recent trends and how to prevent addiction.

Creating a Public Service Announcement About Drug Addiction		
Grade Level: 10		
Planning		**Student Goals**
		● **I can** identify five facts about heroin addiction and explain the impact it has had in my community.
Subject Area(s)		
X	English language arts	● **I can** write a script that critically examines the facts and offer my opinion verbally on the problem of heroin addiction.
	Mathematics	
	Science	● **I can** use the iPad and the iMovie app to create and publish a public service announcement (PSA).
	Social studies	
X	Other: Health	
Language Skills		**Activating Prior Knowledge**
X	Listening	Briefly describe recent current events in the United States regarding the dramatic increase of heroin use among teenagers. Explain how this trend has become an epidemic. Provide curated online resources to students. Help them research facts surrounding this trend.
X	Speaking	
X	Reading	
X	Writing	
X	Viewing	

(Continued)

(Continued)

Resources and Supports		Create QR codes for each link to access the resources easily.
X	Technology tools	
X	Native language	**Engagement**
X	Visuals, realia, manipulatives	*Working in groups:*
X	Graphic organizers	1. Scan the QR codes to take you to the researched resources.
Interaction-Grouping		2. Read the articles and select five quotes, statistics, or details to include in your public service announcement.
	Individual practice	
	Pairs	3. Prepare a storyboard to outline the sequence and illustrations for your PSA.
X	Small group	
	Whole group	4. Write a script for the PSA. Include citations.
X	Online collaboration	5. Use your iPad camera to record your PSA, edit your video using iMovie.

Template adapted from WIDA Lesson Plan Share Space

https://www.wida.us/professionaldev/educatorresources/lessonPlan-shareSpace.aspx

CONSIDER THIS

Visually Representing

English learners can produce a visual product to demonstrate understanding through digital media resources. Students can collect and organize information and record a video that can be authentically published and shared with an audience via YouTube. Consider the five levels of language proficiency and the potential of visual representation for new learning at each of the levels.

DIGITAL AGE EXPLORER'S CORNER

Responding to Literature Collaboratively With E-Publishing

An excellent example of e-publishing in the classroom using the iPad was created by teacher Annette Schidler with a group of 60 ELs who created a book titled *Surviving in Amityville: A Guide Written by Middle School English Language Learners for all English Language Learners*.

While reading the book *Swiss Family Robinson* students discussed the themes of adaptation and survival (Tyrell, 2011). They connected the themes to their own experiences as newcomers in Amityville. Every student had a story to tell and advice to offer.

Then the students collaborated on the survival guide. Each chapter provides each student's unique perspective and advice. The end result is an 11-chapter book that includes video and photos. The e-book is an authentic published work now available through iTunes. A writing project such as this is a good example of the modification of a traditional task.

CHAPTER SUMMARY

Multimedia projects engage all five language skills: listening, speaking, reading, writing, and viewing.

Multimedia projects require ELs to use higher-order thinking skills to shift from consumers to creators of digital content.

Academic content and language learning are scaffolded by the inclusion of audio, video, and images.

Multimedia projects provide an alternative way for ELs to demonstrate knowledge.

The SAMR model can be used to integrate technology to create a transformative classroom that redefines student tasks.

The creation of multimedia content in cooperative learning settings can help ELs develop literacy skills.

PLN QUESTIONS

1. Describe the higher-order skills involved when ELs create multimedia projects.

2. How does the creation of multimedia projects support language learning?

3. How do the roles of teachers and students change when the emphasis is placed on digital content creation?

4. How can the SAMR model help teachers to transform the learning environment for their ELs?

5 Flipping the Classroom for English Learners

Which activities that do not require my physical presence can be shifted out of the class in order to give more class time to activities that are enhanced by my presence? (Bergmann & Sams, 2012, p. 96)

OVERVIEW

In this chapter, you will learn about the benefits of flipping your classroom in order to support students' language and content acquisition and to provide more time for your English learners to interact with their peers in class. The flipped classroom instructional model is a blended learning approach that can empower English learners by providing access to subject matter through customized, teacher-created video tutorials. The direct-instruction video tutorial is used to deliver content that would typically be delivered in class by the teacher through a lecture format. Students direct their own learning by viewing the subject matter independently and then coming to class prepared to ask questions and problem solve with their classmates. We discuss the many ways this instructional model benefits English learners. Ultimately, by flipping the classroom for English learners, they will have more opportunity to think critically in English and to use English to connect authentically with others in order to acquire knowledge. This is perhaps the most important advantage of the flipped classroom for ELs.

DIGITAL AGE LEARNING EXPERIENCE

Getting Ready to Flip

Flipping the classroom does require careful preparation. In the beginning teachers must decide if they would like to create their own direct-instruction tutorials or use premade video resources. It's also important to know that there is more than one way to "flip." The model itself is adjustable, and many variations for delivering the flipped method have emerged as more teachers explore this practice in their own classroom. It is up to teachers to choose how to best implement flipping for their students.

Some variations include the following:

Flipped project-based learning. Students view a series of videos on a real-world problem and collaborate on a project that seeks a solution.

Flipped mastery. Individualized video tutorials are targeted and informed by data. Students work independently and advance to the next topic only after achieving mastery.

Flipped intervention or enrichment. Video tutorials are created to address the specific remediation needs of the student or to allow the student to expand his or her knowledge of the content.

Flipped peer instruction. Students create video tutorials to assist their peers in learning content. Peers work together to complete classroom assignments.

CREATING VIDEOS

Recording screencasts and other types of direct-instruction video tutorials takes time, but doing so allows teachers to scaffold and differentiate the content for the unique language needs of ELs. Whether teachers make their own screencasts or use premade videos in a flipped classroom, teachers and students are ultimately rewarded with more time to explore, interact, and learn.

Some teachers prefer to use video resources from content providers like Discovery Education or Khan Academy, whereas other teachers are flipping "purists" and prefer to create their own videos. There are advantages to both.

Using quality prerecorded videos can help illustrate concepts in an engaging and effective way and can save time. On the other hand, a lot of time can be lost searching online for the perfect video.

By creating a video of yourself providing the instruction, you can increase the amount of "face" time that you have with students. Also, making your own video allows the content to be aligned exactly to what is happening in your classroom. Over time you will build a library of videos to draw from.

There are some basic guidelines when preparing to flip a lesson or a unit of instruction. The length of video should vary according to your students' grade level. It has been suggested that teachers record no more than 1 minute of video instruction per student grade level. In other words, a viewing assignment should not exceed 12 minutes for your high school students. For elementary students, the viewing assignment should not exceed 6 minutes.

SHARING VIDEOS

There are many ways to share or post videos for student viewing. Some teachers upload their videos to YouTube and post the link on their classroom website, whereas others use online learning management platforms like Edmodo or Google Classroom to share and assign videos. You can also create DVDs to give to students who do not have computer access at home. At the end of this chapter there is a list of resources to explore for creating and sharing videos. No matter which method you choose, be sure to inform parents about flipped instruction and the viewing assignment, and tell them how they can help students locate the video online.

After posting the video, give students ample viewing time and scaffolded vocabulary, guiding questions for comprehension, and graphic organizers for fact collecting. It is better to post several videos at a time to allow students to go ahead or go back according to their needs.

ENGAGING STUDENTS IN THE CLASSROOM

Remember that watching video is only one part of a well-planned flipped learning experience. The video is just the beginning of this engaging instructional model. Careful consideration must be given to the activities prepared by the teacher to help students synthesize and apply the information once they have completed the viewing assignment.

One key to a successful flipped classroom is incorporating learning activities that are differentiated and hands-on and require students to apply what they have learned through their at-home viewing. The seed lessons at the end of this chapter provide ideas for developing engaging activities for students.

Figure 5.1 The Flipped Classroom

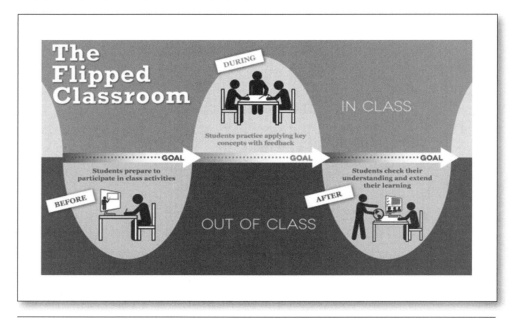

http://ctl.utexas.edu/teaching

The infographic above (Figure 5.1) from the Learning Sciences department at the University of Texas at Austin illustrates the workflow pattern in a flipped learning environment.

TRACKING STUDENT PROGRESS

Many online platforms track electronically whether a student has viewed the video at home. Ultimately, a quick comprehension check at the beginning of class may oftentimes be all the information a teacher needs. Just like any homework assignment, some students will need to be reminded that the viewing must be completed in order for the student to participate in class activities. Student assessment will vary based on the activities designed for each lesson or unit of instruction. Teachers can track student progress using traditional assessments such as test and quizzes, or they can create rubrics and maintain electronic portfolios to store documents and student-created videos. Videos are a wonderful way for ELs to demonstrate both content mastery and language skills. All activities should align to your school's learning standards. In addition, consider the technology standards that your flipped lesson will address.

UNDERSTANDING ELs

Although flipping the classroom is a vastly expanding practice, it is just emerging to support ELs (see www .flippedclassroom.org). Although there might be limited research on the positive impact flipping has on learning for ELs, the anticipated outcomes are substantial when considering research-informed and classroom evidence-based practices. Flipped learning, by definition, requires technology use outside the classroom. Survey your students prior to initiating a flipped classroom to find out what technology tools are available at home to complete a video or web-based task prior to coming to class. Be prepared to offer alternative ways for ELs to complete the flipped task if they do not have access to a computer or other device at home. Establish a buddy system or a flipped learning afterschool club if students cannot complete the task alone due to lack of access to technology devices. Explore options including the school library or computer center or the local public library where students may complete their assignment. Videos may also be created for parents, in their home language, so that they can assist their child.

Digital learning environments support the International Society for Technology in Education Standards for Teachers ISTE 3. a–d:

3. Model Digital Age Work and Learning

   Teachers exhibit knowledge, skills, and work processes representative of an innovative professional in a global and digital society.

   a. Demonstrate fluency in technology systems and the transfer of current knowledge to new technologies and situations.

   b. Collaborate with students, peers, parents, and community members using digital tools and resources to support student success and innovation.

   c. Communicate relevant information and ideas effectively to students, parents, and peers using a variety of digital age media and formats.

   d. Model and facilitate effective use of current and emerging digital tools to locate, analyze, evaluate, and use information resources to support research and learning.

SOURCE: International Society for Technology in Education (2016).

FLIPPING THE CLASSROOM FOR ELs

For English language learners, the flipped model has some obvious advantages. While exploring web-based, multimedia resources such as watching a video prior to class (at home, in the school or public library, in an afterschool center or homework club), students can take notes, work at their own pace, pause and rewind the clip, and rewatch the video as many times as necessary. Watching carefully selected videos naturally lends itself to language learning because the visual content is more readily accessible to students of all proficiency levels than complex textbook syntax and vocabulary.

The next day, teachers can spend less time lecturing in the front of the room and have more time to spend engaged with students, giving more personalized instruction. Students apply the information from the video to complete a project or learning task. Teachers become facilitators in this interactive student-centered environment in which ELs have more processing time and more opportunities to develop academic oral and written communication skills. Using class time to complete tasks collaboratively gives ELs more time to synthesize their learning and practice language with their peers.

When English learners regularly interact with their peers in class, the opportunity to think critically and to use English to connect authentically with others in order to acquire knowledge increases dramatically. Whereas this is perhaps the most important advantage of the flipped classroom for ELs, using multimedia when delivering instruction for ELs also helps them build background knowledge, master vocabulary, infer meaning, and extend their knowledge of a topic.

Although there are many ways to incorporate a flipped learning model for ELs, the benefits are similar. Flipping the ELD/ESL classroom accomplishes the following:

- Allows for asynchronous instruction while extending learning beyond the confines of the classroom and the school day
- Allows for differentiating instruction through tiered flipped experiences before and during class time
- Makes learning visible in the classroom as students explore the topic and use language more deeply following the out-of-class learning experience
- Allows more time for immediate teacher feedback on content and language development in class
- Fosters self-motivated, self-directed learning and curiosity in students

ESSENTIAL PEDAGOGICAL COMPONENTS SUPPORTED BY THE FLIPPED CLASSROOM

Building on growing classroom-based evidence, it is our belief that flipped learning can contribute to the following critical components of effective instruction for ELs.

Establishing Learning Targets
for Content, Language, and Technology

A learning target is "the lesson-sized chunk of information, skills, and reasoning processes that students will come to know deeply and thoroughly" (Moss & Brookhart, 2012, p. 164). Flipped learning requires that teachers share the learning target with their students so they understand what concepts and/or skills will be developed as a result of their independent video or web-based learning and the follow-up in-class work. To formulate learning targets as "I can . . ." statements is highly beneficial for ELs because they have to be able to articulate the outcomes of the learning activity and state the evidence of learning in their own words. The WIDA (2012) *I can descriptors* could be especially helpful for deciding on reasonable expectations for each grade level cluster and for each language proficiency. The WIDA consortium's (see www.wida.us) mission centers around creating quality standards and assessments, conducting research, and offering professional development for educators to advance academic language development and academic achievement for linguistically diverse students. More specifically, a recent WIDA (2014) position paper points out that

> there is now general agreement that all students are learning to manage new sociocultural and language routines in classrooms and schools and that in each content area, students make use of specialized vocabulary, grammar, language functions and related discourse structures, and text types. (para. 1)

WIDA's can-do philosophy indicates a deep belief in the assets and the potential—rather than the deficiencies—of linguistically diverse students.

Activating Students' Prior Knowledge

In the Report of the National Reading Panel (National Institute of Child Health and Human Development [NICHD], 2000), it was noted that "the data suggest that text comprehension is enhanced when readers actively relate the ideas represented in print to their own knowledge and experience and construct mental representations in memory" (p. 14). When students have the opportunity to relate their own personal knowledge and experiences to new learning, content attainment is more successful. Further, Luis Moll (1992) claims that integrating students' *funds of knowledge*—"essential cultural practices and bodies of knowledge and information that households use to survive, to get ahead, or to thrive" (p. 21)—is essential to offer them a foundation for learning based on prior experiences with their immediate and extended family, their community, and their culture.

However, when ELs lack knowledge and experiences related to the core content curriculum, the flipped experience can help them be better prepared for instruction that directly builds on the flipped learning. Robert Marzano (2004) also suggests that building background knowledge "should be at the top of any list of interventions intended to enhance student achievement" (p. 4), whereas Doug Fisher and Nancy Frey (2009) expressed urgency when stating that "background knowledge simply has to become an instructional focus if we want to help students make sense of school. We will lose a generation of learners if we don't act now" (p. 20). Flipping the classroom can substantially contribute to building the much-needed background knowledge for ELs to cope with the rigor of the curriculum.

Building Academic Language

Jeff Zwiers (2004–2005) observed that

academic language is the linguistic glue that holds the tasks, texts, and tests of school together. If students can't use this glue well, their academic work is likely to fall apart. I define *academic language* as the set of words and phrases that (1) describe content-area knowledge and procedures, (2) express complex thinking processes and abstract concepts, and (3) create cohesion and clarity in written and oral discourse. (p. 60)

Classroom interactions are more productive when students come to class having exposure to the key concepts and ideas and understanding key words and phrases that the teacher and their peers are going to use. Beck, McKeown, and Kucan (2013) found that key features of effective vocabulary instruction "are frequent and varied encounters with target words and robust instructional activities that engage students in deep processing" (p. 83). Flipped learning offers multiple encounters with vocabulary and allows for meaningful engagement with the new content during class time.

Making Content Accessible

Carefully selected or creatively produced teacher-made video clips offer a visual window to understanding. Through video viewing, complex content becomes more accessible because students can see and hear critical information illustrated on the screen. Make sure the narrator is clear and easy to understand or record the videos yourself to ensure the appropriate speed of speech. If closed-captioning is available, in addition to seeing images, diagrams, authentic examples, and other concrete supports for the spoken word, ELs can also follow the script at the bottom of the screen as they watch the video, thus receiving yet another channel of input. When ELs have access to a variety of multimodal and multimedia resources that make concepts clear, their comprehension of the target content increases and their receptive language skills expand as well (Echevarria, Vogt, & Short, 2012). Digital tools such as EDpuzzle and Zaption allow you to embed comprehension questions within your own video or premade videos that you find on sites like YouTube or TED-Ed.

Enhancing Student Engagement

Jonathan Bergmann and Aaron Sams (2012) ask one critical question in their book on flipped learning: "What is the use of face-to-face time with students?" ELs undoubtedly need opportunities to engage more with the language, explore the content more actively, and interact with all members of the classroom community: English-speaking peer models and fellow ELs as well as teachers, paraprofessionals, instructional aides, and volunteers who might be present in the classroom.

It is well-established that language learning takes place in a sociocultural context (Gottlieb & Ernst-Slavin, 2014). Holtgraves (2002) observed that "to use language is to perform an action, and it is a meaningful action, with consequences for the speaker, the hearer, and the conversation of which it is part" (p. 5). Varied grouping configurations that allow for both heterogeneous and homogenous interactions in pairs, triads, small groups, large groups, or teams as well as in whole-class settings lead to more conversations and engaged learning for ELs. Capitalizing on bilingual peer bridges—students who speak the same native language—teachers create opportunities for peer-to-peer support in the shared language, whereas heterogeneous grouping affords more exposure to peer models and clarifications as well as co-construction of meaning with English-speaking peers.

MAKE-IT-YOUR-OWN LESSON SEEDS

The following brief overviews provide a topic with "seed" ideas that we invite you to "grow" into a full lesson plan for your classroom.

Informational Text for Tiered Writing

The following lesson is intended to explain and demonstrate how ELs can be supported in English language arts (ELA) through scaffolded strategies and technology that encourage language learning and content learning while applying

(Continued)

(Continued)

information and practicing language with their peers. This ELA lesson seed for fourth-graders structures opportunities for students to use the communication skills of listening, speaking, reading, and writing in a variety of ways that allow English learners to acquire the skills needed to be successful in the classroom.

Informational Text for Tiered Writing	
Grade Level: 4	

Planning		Student Goals
Subject Area(s)		<ul><li>**I can** read and comprehend informational text and use text evidence to demonstrate understanding of a topic.</li><li>**I can** formulate prewriting questions and organize information and ideas using graphic organizers to write a researched topic.</li><li>**I can** use electronic and print resources to research, plan, and construct an informational text writing topic and post on the class webpage (WordPress).</li></ul>
X	English language arts	
	Mathematics	
X	Science	
	Social studies	
	Other:	
Language Skills		**Activating Prior Knowledge**
X	Listening	
X	Speaking	Discuss the assigned homework video viewing assignment (learnzillion.com). Brainstorm and generate language to discuss your writing topics.
X	Reading	
X	Writing	
X	Viewing	
Resources and Supports		**Engagement**
X	Technology tools	
X	Native language	<ul><li>Identify what questions you have about your writing topic by completing the graphic organizer.</li><li>Research your writing topic using electronic and print resources.</li><li>Organize your information in a table of contents using the information gathered from your research and graphic organizer.</li><li>Draft writing projects must include details to express ideas clearly and textual features such as diagrams, charts, and visuals.</li><li>Revise and edit your final draft project for publication on the class webpage.</li></ul>
X	Visuals, realia, manipulatives	
X	Graphic organizers	
Interaction-Grouping		
X	Individual practice	
X	Pairs	
X	Small group	
X	Whole group	
X	Online collaboration	

Template adapted from WIDA Lesson Plan Share Space
https://www.wida.us/professionaldev/educatorresources/lessonPlan-shareSpace.aspx

"What If" History Project

The sample lesson we chose for this chapter is an alternate history project, or counterfactual history project. The counterfactual history project requires students to investigate an event or period in time. Students must do thorough research and then identify a specific moment in history from which to create a point of divergence that ultimately changes the outcome of the event. The point of divergence can be when a student imagines a historical figure making a different decision or it can occur when the circumstances of an event are changed by the student, impacting the historical record. This project offers English learners the opportunity to work collaboratively with their peers by using technology tools to research actual historical events, describe and explain the point of divergence, and create a timeline of these newly imagined events in history.

"What If" History Project		
Grade Level: 11		
Planning		**Student Goals**
Subject Area(s)		• **I can** identify a different point of view in the civil rights movement and explain how individuals and systems create and sustain change.
X	English language arts	• **I can** narrate a newly created event in history in the past-perfect tense and use main ideas and supporting evidence in verbal and written format.
	Mathematics	
	Science	• **I can** use primary and secondary sources such as digital, print, and visual materials to research history and create a multimedia presentation.
X	Social studies	
	Other:	
Language Skills		**Activating Prior Knowledge**
X	Listening	Assign a video clip of Dr. King's "I Have a Dream" speech for at-home viewing. Briefly discuss the video viewing assignment the next day and encourage students to brainstorm and generate language to discuss the civil rights movement.
X	Speaking	
X	Reading	
X	Writing	
X	Viewing	
Resources and Supports		
X	Technology tools	
X	Native language	**Engagement**
X	Visuals, realia, manipulatives	*Working in groups*
X	Graphic organizers	1. Identify specifically a point during the civil rights movement in which you are interested in changing the outcome.

(Continued)

(Continued)

Interaction-Grouping		2. Read background information on the history leading up to and immediately following the point in the civil rights movement you are interested in changing. Also research information on the impact that this event had on today's society.
	Individual practice	
	Pairs	
X	Small group	
	Whole group	
X	Online collaboration	

2. Read background information on the history leading up to and immediately following the point in the civil rights movement you are interested in changing. Also research information on the impact that this event had on today's society.

3. Identify two events that happened immediately before the point of divergence, and find two primary-source documents related to those events.

4. Between the point of divergence and the present time, introduce two imaginary "new" events to the timeline.

5. Describe each of these new events and create your own primary-source documents as evidence of each event. Primary sources can be a journal, newspaper article, speech, photograph, law, bill, court case, cartoon, or other document.

6. Create a multimedia presentation. The finished product must include the real and imaginary events, the new primary-source documents you created, and the story of life in America today as a result of the changes you have chosen to make.

Template adapted from WIDA Lesson Plan Share Space

https://www.wida.us/professionaldev/educatorresources/lessonPlan-shareSpace.aspx

CONSIDER THIS

Make sure you scaffold and differentiate both flipped content and the in-class project-based or task-based learning according to ELs' proficiency levels. Students whose receptive language skills are still emerging benefit from shorter digital content that is rich in visual input and has closed-captioning added.

DIGITAL AGE EXPLORER'S CORNER

Flipping One Lesson at a Time

It can be difficult to know how to start flipping. The easiest way to begin can be with a single lesson. This is what happened at Southside

High School in Rockville Centre, New York. One day, the students in the intermediate ELD/ESL classroom were reading *Their Eyes Were Watching God* by Zora Neale Hurston for their English class. The ELD/ESL teacher had been showing scenes from the movie in class to aid student comprehension of the book, but it was very time consuming. She decided to adapt a lesson that she had already created on finding textual evidence and incorporate a home viewing assignment.

The next day students came to class and were asked to read four separate plot overviews and find evidence in the text in order to answer comprehension questions. Then, over 2 days using iPads, they created short screencasts to illustrate what they had learned. By viewing the video at home, not only did the students have a better understanding of the book, but they had more time in class to create and use their English language skills. Now the ELD/ESL teacher includes flipped lessons as part of her curriculum throughout the year.

CHAPTER SUMMARY

A flipped class is one that inverts the typical cycle of content acquisition and application.

Flipped learning is beneficial to ELs because they can access content and gain necessary knowledge before class through a viewing assignment.

Teachers guide ELs to interactively clarify information, apply knowledge during class, and practice language with their peers.

Teachers prepare learning opportunities that are tiered according to language and academic proficiency levels.

ELs guide their own learning by preparing questions and completing tasks independently.

Teachers anticipate where students need the most help and act as the "guide on the side."

Learning becomes visible for teachers and students during classroom collaboration.

Teachers guide the process with immediate feedback and mini tutorials using new language and home language as necessary.

Students continue applying their knowledge and skills after clarification and feedback.

Teachers provide additional explanations and resources as necessary to make content more accessible to ELs.

Teachers assess ELs' language and content proficiency through a variety of formative and summative assessments.

PLN QUESTIONS

1. What are your objectives when using videos with English learners? How would you incorporate these videos in a flipped learning environment?

2. When evaluating premade video resources to support your English learners in the content areas, what features are most important to you?

3. What lesson delivery benefits can teacher-made videos provide you as an educator? What benefits do teacher-made videos provide to ELs?

4. What types of instructional activities can be provided to ELs during the video viewing assignment?

5. After the viewing assignment, how do you support ELs and encourage student interaction during in-class activities?

6 Collaboration and Communication

Collaborative projects were once seen as somewhat of a novelty, but now are essential for working in the Internet age. Technology has made work location relatively meaningless . . . a 21st century classroom looks to engage learners in collaborative groups, where learning takes place in and out of school. (Covili, 2012, p. 3)

OVERVIEW

In this chapter, we discuss leveraging digital tools to increase collaboration and communication for ELs in the classroom and beyond. According to "Preparing 21st Century Students for a Global Society: An Educator's Guide to the 'Four C's,'" 21st century readers and writers need to "build relationships with others to pose and solve problems collaboratively and cross-culturally" as well as "develop proficiency with the tools of technology" (NEA, p. 16). If we want equitable access to education for our ELs, it is essential for today's English learner to work with others in both face-to-face and virtual collaborative settings. Collaboration increases opportunities for language development and authentic peer interaction. In addition, collaborating online promotes digital literacy and increases opportunities for teachers to provide targeted, personalized instruction.

Whenever possible, choose online collaboration tools that are "device agnostic" so that students can readily access them from whichever device they have outside of the classroom. To establish a support system for ELs who might have limited access to technology or emerging skills to use such tools, set up study buddies or invite them to form study teams for homework or out-of-class projects. Encourage students to use locally available resources such as community centers and public libraries.

According to Prensky (2010), in a collaborative learning environment, teachers become goal setters, facilitators, and analyzers. His description of "partnering pedagogy" can provide a basis for digital-age EL instruction that incorporates technology to facilitate communication and workflow. In this environment, using learning management systems (LMS) allows students to engage in personalized language learning while interacting with others in online discussions. Cloud-based productivity tools allow students to brainstorm together and write collaboratively online, and teachers can provide personalized or group feedback on language and content by posting comments and offering suggestions for revision.

Partnering pedagogy in a collaborative environment such as this requires that students become self-directed learners. We discuss the planning and stage setting that must occur in order to create a safe and productive space for students to collaborate and communicate inside and outside of the classroom.

DIGITAL AGE LEARNING EXPERIENCE

The 5 C's for 21st Century Learning

Collaborative learning is not a new concept, but with the technology now available, teachers and teacher leaders can go even further than before to design collaborative projects that promote language learning and increase communication between ELs and their peers. As a result of the digital age, we now have the tools we need to allow true collaboration to continue when the school day is over. Students can work together wherever and whenever they have Internet access.

An example of this type of collaborative project has been designed by Heather Miller, director of LPM Education. She created a collaborative, interdisciplinary digital humanities project that offers a new model for high school social studies research. A social studies project such as this can be especially helpful to English learners because they often struggle with U.S. history due to not having the same background knowledge a student raised in the United States has acquired. This project allows students to access U.S. history by conducting real-world research with scholars as well as develop language skills while collaborating with peers from various schools to analyze and present their findings.

Whaling History is a three-unit program for 10th- and 11th-grade U.S. history students. The project was implemented among three high schools, one in Hawaii and two in New York (Long Island and Lower Manhattan). Each school researched their local whaling history and its impact on the development of their own community. Then the three schools compared and contrasted their histories and linked them to broader historical trends. To learn more about this innovative project, visit http://www.lepagemiller.com/digital-humanities-1.html.

This type of interaction is directly aligned with the goals of the Partnership for 21st Century Learning mentioned in Chapter 1. The National Education Association (NEA) developed the Partnership for 21st Century Learning (www.p21.org) in 2002 in order to advocate 21st century readiness for every student. They have identified four specific 21st century skills as most important for K–12 learners. These skills became known as the 4 C's—critical thinking, communication, collaboration, and creativity. The 4 C's can be readily integrated into instructional practices for ELs and enhanced by adding a fifth C for culture.

Critical thinking. Linking learning across subjects and disciplines and assisting ELs in developing background knowledge. Using technology to reduce or remove language barriers so that ELs can decipher problems and find solutions.

Communication. Providing numerous opportunities for ELs to share thoughts, ask questions, and discuss ideas and solutions with their peers. This could include the use of translation apps, video chats, and online discussion boards.

Collaboration. Creating projects that allow ELs to work with classmates both in class and virtually to achieve a shared goal, while contributing their own talent and expertise. This may require the use of tiered tasks and scaffolded assignments.

Creativity. Helping ELs express their thoughts, ideas, and content knowledge creatively. This can be achieved through the use of multimedia resources and "gold standard" project-based learning activities that help ELs use the target language to make real-life connections to learning.

Culture. Recognizing that ELs bring rich cultural and linguistic experiences to the classroom and building on them. It is essential that ELs make meaningful connections between the home and school cultures and develop bicultural identities. Design collaborative projects that demonstrate an acceptance and appreciation for cultural diversity. This involves including the global community and respecting the needs of those who are collaborating from different cultures, building an awareness for all students of how culture impacts an individual's or group's choices, and providing a forum for discussions related to multiculturalism.

PROVIDE SYNCHRONOUS AND ASYNCHRONOUS LEARNING EXPERIENCES

There are many digital tools to craft and design the classroom platform from which we want to launch ELs into collaborative learning. The following resources and tools make student collaboration easy any time and anywhere there is an Internet connection.

- Google Apps for Education (GAFE)

  ○ Use Google Drive and Google Docs for collaborative writing tasks.
  ○ Use Google Classroom to create and post assignments, share comments, and work in a paperless environment. Google Classroom is part of GAFE, which includes Drive, Docs, Sheets, Forms, Slides, and Gmail as well as many other useful Google tools and add-ons.

- Backchannels and lesson boards: 81DASH, TodaysMeet, Realtime-Board, Blendspace, Tackk

  ○ Take notes, post questions, and brainstorm on projects in real time while simultaneously collaborating face-to-face. Access information, post comments, and continue to brainstorm when you are not together.

- Learning management systems: Moodle, iTunes U, Canvas, Desire2Learn, BrainHoney

  ○ Post multimedia assignments and discussion threads and create project pages. Build and publish a multimedia syllabus, track assignments, and manage notes. Hold online discussions. Enroll in courses from all around the world. Includes K–12 and higher education as well as institutions such as the Smithsonian and NASA.

- Video chatting: Google Hangouts, FaceTime, Skype, FieldTripZoom

  ○ Quick and easy way to collaborate virtually in real time as a class or for peer tutoring from anywhere there is an Internet connection.

- QR codes
  - QR codes save time and make sharing online resources simple. Teachers can curate online resources and guide students to useful sites or documents. They are used to create scavenger hunts and to showcase student projects in gallery walks. They are also a great way to share links with parents.

UNDERSTANDING ELs

Applebee, Langer, Nystrand, and Gamoran (2003) emphasized the positive outcomes of interactive, discussion-based learning on what they referred to as nonmainstream students—low achievers, children of the poor, and second-language learners. As opposed to sitting and trying to learn in a traditional classroom environment, they noted that linguistically and academically diverse learners

> do much better when instruction builds on previous knowledge and current ideas and experiences, permits students to voice their understandings and refine them through substantive discussion with others, and explicitly provides the new knowledge and strategies that students need to participate successfully in the continuing discussion. (p. 689)

Using digital tools for collaboration supports student participation: communication skills develop both in face-to-face settings and via virtual connections such as backchannels TodaysMeet and 81DASH. These websites allow students to

Virtual collaboration supports the International Society for Technology in Education Standards for Teachers ISTE 1. a–d:

1. Facilitate and Inspire Student Learning and Creativity

   Teachers use their knowledge of subject matter, teaching and learning, and technology to facilitate experiences that advance student learning, creativity, and innovation in both face-to-face and virtual environments.

   a. Promote, support, and model creative and innovative thinking and inventiveness.

   b. Engage students in exploring real-world issues and solving authentic problems using digital tools and resources.

   c. Promote student reflection using collaborative tools to reveal and clarify students' conceptual understanding and thinking, planning, and creative processes.

   d. Model collaborative knowledge construction by engaging in learning with students, colleagues, and others in face-to-face and virtual environments.

SOURCE: International Society for Technology in Education (2016).

expand class conversation online and post comments, questions, and resources instantaneously while engaged in a face-to-face class discussion.

Technology offers a wide-open platform for teacher collaboration, as well as collaboration among students. You can also use digital collaboration tools to enhance parent engagement. Use Google Forms to receive feedback from parents. Keep communication open with families and inform them of school activities and student progress by sharing students' work on your school webpage or classroom blog. Be sure to provide opportunities for students to access the Internet when outside the classroom. Some districts even provide community access to the Internet. Telecommunication companies such as Verizon provide support and information and offer grants for these initiatives.

INTERACTION

Vygotsky (1978) is most known for establishing that learning is a process occurring through interaction between people in social, cultural, and historical contexts. Positioning students as thinkers who process and generate new ideas while interacting with others is critical. Among others, Roskos, Tabors, and Lenhart (2009) also concluded that "children's speaking and listening skills lead the way for their reading and writing skills, and together these language skills are the primary tools of the mind for all future learning" (p. vii). Classroom interaction and collaboration are critical for all learning to take place. Lauren Resnick and her team of researchers at the University of Pittsburgh Institute for Learning have developed a set of talk moves known as Accountable Talk. Michaels, O'Connor, Hall, and Resnick (2010) defined what makes talk accountable: "For classroom talk to promote learning it must be accountable: to the learning community, to accurate and appropriate knowledge, and to rigorous thinking" (p. 1).

What does it mean for ELs? To support cognitive, academic, and linguistic development, ELs need the following:

- Instructional conversations (Goldenberg, 1992; Tharp & Gallimore, 1991) and other academic interaction frameworks that recognize and support ELs as autonomous thinkers who are actively engaged in the learning process along with their teachers and peers.
- Classrooms transformed into a "community of learners" (Tharp & Gallimore, 1991, p. 5) where the verbal traffic is not controlled by the

teachers (Cazden, 2001); instead all learners contribute to discussing and solving authentic problems.

- Conversation protocols that are modeled, explicitly taught, scaffolded, and practiced. For example, Zwiers and Crawford (2009) emphasized the importance of teaching ELs to do the following:

  ○ Paraphrase and summarize
  ○ Elaborate and clarify
  ○ Support one's ideas with details
  ○ Build on or challenge other students' ideas
  ○ Apply their ideas to their own lives

- Similarly, Michaels et al. (2010) suggested student-to-student questioning, probing, and the use of evidence in a typical accountable talk interaction.
- Universal prompts as suggested by Bambrick-Santoyo, Settles, and Worrell (2013). The more ELs hear their teachers apply prompts such as, "Tell me more," "What makes you think that?," "Why do you think that is?," and "Why is this important?" to elicit more student talk, the more likely ELs are going to start using and ultimately internalizing these talk moves and prompts with their peers.
- Socratic circles or formal discussions based on a fiction or nonfiction selection in which the leader of the seminar (the teacher or student) asks the group open-ended questions. ELs learn to listen to each other, think deeply and critically, and articulate their own ideas and offer answers in response to what others have contributed.
- Real talk or engagement in genuine student-to-student discussions (Boyd & Galda (2011). What this means is that ELs need to learn "how to enter into a conversation; how to take turns without explicit permission from [the teacher]; and how to listen to each other so that they could move from individual contributions without much uptake to talk that was truly conversational, with students responding to one another's comments" (Boyd & Galda, 2011, p. 34).

Technology can facilitate this process through the use of virtual meeting rooms such as Google Hangouts, FaceTime, Skype, or FieldTripZoom, where students can communicate face-to-face, in real time, from practically anywhere in the world with Internet access.

FEATURES OF ACCOUNTABLE TALK

Students must be accountable to their learning community by

listening carefully to others,

adding on to what others have stated,

asking questions and seeking proof,

disagreeing respectfully, and

paraphrasing and summarizing.

Students must be accountable to accurate knowledge by

using factual information and providing evidence;

using precise, academic language; and

asking others to provide evidence for their claims.

Students must be accountable to rigorous thinking by

making connections and synthesizing ideas;

making clear statements and providing related evidence;

building justifications, arguments, explanations, and reasons; and

evaluating the claims and arguments of others.

Adapted from the Accountable Talk Sourcebook (Michaels et al., 2010).

COOPERATIVE LEARNING

Cooperative learning has also been widely used in classrooms with English learners as well as with all learners at all grade levels. Johnson and Johnson (1999), Slavin (1995), and others have found cooperative learning to lead to stronger peer motivation, active student engagement, and increased achievement while also providing opportunities for meaningful communication and oral language development for at-risk learners (McGroarty, 1993). In his work on visible learning, John Hattie (2012) identified peer interactions and peer support as having positive impact on learning and socializing into the school culture. Hattie specifically suggested that cooperative learning is most powerful after the students have acquired sufficient surface knowledge to then be involved in discussion and learning with peers—usually in some structured manner. It is then most useful for learning concepts, verbal problem-solving, categorizing, spatial problem-solving, retention and memory, and guessing-judging-predicting. (pp. 78–79)

If we want ELs to develop language and literacy skills as well as new understanding in the content areas, we need to offer them ample opportunities for processing information and for using their new language through interaction and collaboration with their peers. To become successful collaborators, they need to work in groups of all sizes: in pairs, in triads, small groups, larger teams, and whole-class discussion.

Varied group configurations and flexible grouping strategies will ensure that ELs learn to cooperate with a range of peers without seeing themselves and others as belonging to static groups. Depending on the goals and objectives of the lesson and the technology tools involved, ELs can work well in both heterogeneously and homogeneously designed groups. As Parker (2006) noted, the classroom is the place for the much-needed "social occasions that provide opportunities for discussants to think, speak, listen, and learn together, with and across their differences, about a specified topic" (p. 11).

Newly arrived ELs face multiple challenges as they begin their education in U.S. schools. They need opportunities for simultaneously developing oral language proficiency and essential skills and content to make progress toward grade-level expectations as well as learning about cultural norms and customs in their school, community, and county of residence. Using translation apps such as Google Translate, Tabletop, or Talking Translator can support oral communication.

The use of technology for collaboration plays an important role in helping students take more responsibility for their participation within authentic contexts. Technology also serves as a scaffolding tool so that no matter the proficiency level or what language is spoken in the classroom a student can take initiative and contribute to the group task. For example, while reading within a platform such as Newsela, the teacher can adjust settings so that the text will match each student's appropriate Lexile level. Long-term ELs who have not made adequate progress in their language acquisition often have strong bilingual oral language skills. They may have even developed native-like fluency in English. Their literacy skills both in the native language and English are significantly less developed than their oral skills are. A priority for these learners is targeted literacy instruction in both languages, so written communication and collaborative work using digital tools will substantially contribute to accelerating their learning.

MAKE-IT-YOUR-OWN LESSON SEEDS

The following brief overviews provide a topic with "seed" ideas that we invite you to "grow" into a full lesson plan for your classroom.

Photosynthesis and the Cellular Respiration Cycle

In the following lesson seed, students will learn that plants release oxygen during the process of photosynthesis by using nutrients from the soil and carbon dioxide and sunlight from the air to make sugar that plants use for food. They will explore the photosynthesis process and the relationship between plants and animals in the cellular respiration cycle. Students will work in groups to formulate questions, conduct research, construct and test their hypothesis, draw conclusions, and communicate their results using Google Classroom and Google Apps for Education (GAFE). This lesson can be modified for use with other online learning management systems if your school is not enrolled in GAFE.

Photosynthesis and the Cellular Respiration Cycle

Grade Level: 5

Planning		Student Goals
Subject Area(s)		• **I can** read informational text using digital resources and compare and contrast what animals need to survive and what plants need to survive.
X	English language arts	• **I can** formulate questions, write a hypothesis, and write my conclusions based on my experiment.
	Mathematics	• **I can** create, complete, and collaborate with my teacher and classmates using electronic documents to record scientific results.
X	Science	
	Social studies	
	Other:	
Language Skills		**Activating Prior Knowledge**
X	Listening	Explain how all living things get their energy from the sun and describe photosynthesis and the cellular respiration process by posting a video assignment for students in Google Classroom; include questions for discussion. Discuss what an organism needs for energy and have students brainstorm with a partner what plants need to survive and what animals need to survive. Students identify the relationship between photosynthesis and cellular respiration.
X	Speaking	
X	Reading	
X	Writing	
X	Viewing	
Resources and Supports		
X	Technology tools	
X	Native language	
X	Visuals, realia, manipulatives	
X	Graphic organizers	

Interaction-Grouping		Engagement
	Individual practice	• Formulate questions about how photosynthesis occurs in plants and how cellular respiration occurs in plants and animals.
X	Pairs	
X	Small group	• Post your questions in Google Classroom Stream for online discussion.
	Whole group	• Conduct online research for a scientific experiment to test the photosynthesis and cellular respiration process. (Use QR codes or post links in Google Classroom.)
X	Online collaboration	
		• Construct a hypothesis and test your experiment. Record your findings in a shared Google Doc or Sheets and review comments and questions posed by your classmates and teacher.
		• Draw conclusions and communicate the results of your experiment by presenting your findings using Google Slides.

Template adapted from WIDA Lesson Plan Share Space

https://www.wida.us/professionaldev/educatorresources/lessonPlan-shareSpace.aspx

Creating a Virtual Art Gallery

This lesson seed idea takes students on an Internet scavenger hunt using QR codes to guide them to various websites. They will research famous artists and explore resources such as the Google Cultural Institute and Google Art Project. After completing their research, students will create a student art gallery using the website Artsonia. Each group will focus on a different art movement and must write reflections on each piece of artwork that they create for display. This project allows English learners to think critically about their work and use academic vocabulary to reflect on other students' work as well as their own. Together students will go on virtual tours to visit museums from around the world. They will work collaboratively to create their own gallery exhibit. They will create their own artwork reflective of the art movement and will write a short reflection on the piece. Technology tools such as QR codes, Google Docs, and photo editors will be incorporated into the project. Visitors to the gallery can post comments and give feedback to peers about the artwork they created.

(Continued)

(Continued)

Creating a Virtual Art Gallery	
Grade Level: 9	

Planning		**Student Goals**

Student Goals

- **I can** identify an art movement and explain how a historical time period influences artists' work.
- **I can** write a reflection that critically examines a piece of art and offer my opinion verbally on my own artwork and that of others using general academic vocabulary and art terminology.
- **I can** use the Internet to publish and update individual or shared writing products, taking advantage of technology's capacity to link to other information and to display information flexibly and dynamically.

Subject Area(s)	
X	English language arts
	Mathematics
	Science
	Social studies
X	Other: Art

Language Skills	
X	Listening
X	Speaking
X	Reading
X	Writing
X	Viewing

Activating Prior Knowledge

Model the tasks students will be doing together. Take students on a virtual museum tour via the Google Art Project. Select an artist. Briefly describe the artist and art movement and explain how the movement may have challenged conventional thought at the time. Elicit vocabulary that will help them describe the paintings they will be viewing. Distribute QR codes with various artists and movements for students to explore.

Resources and Supports	
X	Technology tools
X	Native language
X	Visuals, realia, manipulatives
X	Graphic organizers

Interaction-Grouping	
	Individual practice
	Pairs
X	Small group
	Whole group
X	Online collaboration

Engagement

Working in groups with your iPads, follow these steps:

1. Scan the QR codes to take you to the Google Art Project (https://www.google.com/culturalinstitute/project/art-project)

2. Look at several famous paintings by artists within the art movement that your group has selected to develop some essential understanding about the art movement's key styles.

3. Identify two artists who were famous within the art movement.

4. Select four works that define the key styles of the movement and justify your choices.

5. Create your own artwork reflective of the movement.

6. Take a photo of your artwork, edit the picture, and upload to Artsonia for the exhibit.

Reflective Writing

1. What are the key characteristics of the art movement you selected?

2. Which aspects of your artwork do you consider successful and why?

3. What might you like to improve on in your artwork, and how might you do this?

(Adapted from lesson presented by Katie Kelly Art Teacher, Lynbrook UFSD, and Mark Pasciutti, technology staff developer at the LITECH Summit 2014.)

Template adapted from WIDA Lesson Plan Share Space

https://www.wida.us/professionaldev/educatorresources/lessonPlan-shareSpace.aspx

CONSIDER THIS

Parker (2006) suggested that the classroom is the place for "social occasions that provide opportunities for discussants to think, speak, listen, and learn together, with and across their differences, about a specified topic" (p. 11). In what way can we ensure that English learners have a classroom as a safe place to practice language and collaboration skills across the content areas with peers of all language proficiencies?

DIGITAL AGE EXPLORER'S CORNER

Collaboration and Accelerated Learning

Technology director and "lead innovator" at Farmingdale Union Free School District (UFSD), Dr. William Brennan (2013) is serious

(Continued)

(Continued)

about creating a learning environment that supports collaboration both virtually and in the classroom. He firmly believes in the notion of using networked intelligence to accelerate personal and organizational learning. Farmingdale UFSD decided to "go Google" and created a Google Apps for Education account for the district. Having GAFE allows students and teachers to collaborate on the Google platform within their own private Google network. The district is device "agnostic" and encourages the use of multiple devices and platforms to access content and engage in learning. They encourage BYOD (bring your own device) and also use iPads in the ELD/ESL classroom. Virtual communities of practice (VCOP) support teachers, and the district conducts an annual Long Island Connected Educators summit to encourage collaboration among regional educators as well.

CHAPTER SUMMARY

Collaborative learning supports the development of the four +1 language skills for ELs whether in class or while communicating online.

Collaborative learning is beneficial to ELs because they can use the target language with peers to engage in real-world conversation in order to complete an academic task.

Students can publish work to authentic audiences and reflect on their work together through virtual communities.

Teachers can use online learning management systems to track progress, provide feedback, and identify and target the needs of ELs more effectively.

Online collaboration can be synchronous or asynchronous, allowing for access to class assignments and conversations any time.

Teachers can differentiate language and content instruction for ELs by posting comments, video tutorials, and web resources in an online learning management system.

Online collaboration tools model and support college and career readiness skills and accelerate learning.

PLN QUESTIONS

1. Describe the benefits of peer collaboration for ELs.

2. What unique challenges might ELs face in collaborative learning environments?

3. When working outside the classroom, how can technology support ELs to complete a collaborative task?

4. How can online collaboration tools accelerate learning for ELs?

5. Which technology tools do you find most effective to support classroom workflow, collaboration, and communication?

7 Virtual Communities and Digital Citizenship

My kids feel they have friends in different countries, not just fellow students working on a problem. This makes them feel loved, thus making the world feel like a village. Global collaboration promotes peace around the world and makes us work as a team.

—Livingstone Kegode, teacher in Nairobi,
Kenya (Douglas, 2015, p. 27)

OVERVIEW

One of the newest challenges teachers face is to educate students about being responsible digital citizens. Free platforms such as Moodle, Schoology, and Edmodo offer a hybrid of social media and education functions that can be used as learning management systems and to connect with other communities of learners. Teachers are developing creative and useful ways to incorporate popular social media sites like Twitter, Instagram, and Facebook into daily lessons. These networking opportunities expand learning for students beyond the physical classroom. Yet in order to use these tools successfully, we must also teach digital citizenship.

In this chapter, we discuss the term *digital citizenship* and how we can help students become part of a global learning community. Many of our

English learners have experienced what it means to be a citizen in one or more countries, but they may not understand what it means to be a digital citizen. We can expand our students' worldview and provide safety for all of our students by teaching this very important topic explicitly. Expressions such as "self-reflect before you self-reveal" and "pause before you post" are good starting points for the lessons ELs must learn. In conjunction with this, we can create enriched learning experiences by connecting with others throughout the world. The Global Classroom Project (http://theglo balclassroomproject.org) is one example of how collaboration may reach beyond the walls of a classroom, a school, or even a local community. According to this initiative, teachers and students from across the globe share and teach lessons to each other via Skype and YouTube. Students not only practice their language and gain new knowledge about select topics of interest; they also develop intercultural communication and collaboration skills and heightened awareness of global citizenship.

DIGITAL AGE LEARNING EXPERIENCE

Teaching Digital Citizenship

According to Tom Whitby (2014), a connected educator is someone who "embodies a mindset rather than represents someone who does specific things in specific ways" (p. 54). In other words, opening a Skype, Instagram, Twitter, or Facebook account is the first step, but to truly become a connected educator you must model good digital citizenship and use the Internet to share, collaborate, and expand your own knowledge while you teach students how to do the same safely and effectively.

Digital citizenship is a broad term that encompasses many topics related to safe and responsible use of technology and more specifically, digital communication via the Internet. The ISTE Standards for Students describes good digital citizens as "students who understand human, cultural, and societal issues related to technology and practice legal and ethical behavior" (ISTE, 2016). This includes using technology to actively collaborate with peers to meet learning objectives. For ELs, digital communication means more opportunity to increase authentic interaction through the target language and more opportunity to get additional support while learning new concepts. Even students with limited or interrupted formal education (SLIFEs/SIFEs) who are typically characterized as lacking multiple years of formal schooling in their native countries can, nonetheless, participate in virtual communities and online learning activities. Teachers should employ scaffolding techniques that include visual and hands-on learning opportunities for students with emerging or preliteracy skills as well as translanguaging (García, 2009, García & Li, 2014). Using bilingual websites such as http://www.colorincolorado.org can provide resources for educators and parents and allow students to draw on their home language to clarify understanding.

All students must be explicitly taught appropriate online conduct, Internet safety, and how to conduct valid research as part of a fundamental 21st century skill set. Common Sense Media (https://www.commonsensemedia.org/educators/curriculum) has developed a free digital literacy and citizenship curriculum that offers a scope and sequence for Grades K–12 with lesson plans and teacher guides all available in pdf format and through Nearpod and iBooks. These lessons are aligned with both the Common Core Standards and ISTE Standards and even provide resources in Spanish and French. This curriculum is an easy way to start a dialogue with students about digital citizenship. Topics in this scope and sequence include the following:

- *Student privacy and security.* Strategies for managing online information and keeping it secure (such as creating strong passwords and avoiding scams).
- *Digital footprint and reputation.* How to protect your own privacy and respect others' privacy and reminding students to "self-reflect before they self-reveal" as well as understand the permanence of each and every post.
- *Self-image and identity.* Exploring your online versus offline identity.
- *Creative credit and copyright.* Responsibilities and rights as creators and consumers of online content.
- *Relationships and communication.* Interpersonal and intrapersonal skills related to positive online communication and communities.
- *Information and literacy.* The ability to identify, find, evaluate, and use information effectively.
- *Cyberbullying.* What a student should do if involved in a cyberbullying situation.
- *Internet safety.* Collaborating with others worldwide while staying safe. Distinguishing between inappropriate contact and positive connections.

BUILDING BRIDGES THROUGH GLOBAL PROJECT-BASED LEARNING

Good digital citizenship provides the foundation for ELs to embark on global project-based learning and is a natural extension of their personal experiences from various cultures. Project-based learning (PBL) is a teaching method in which students gain knowledge and skills by working for an extended period of time to investigate and respond to a complex question, problem, or challenge. Global PBL involves problem solving for real-world challenges around the globe. In his article "Students Gain Real-Life Insights With Global PBL," author Tim Douglas (2015) highlights how facilitating connections with others through global PBL allows students to not only feel the joy that comes through helping others but also better retain what they have learned. He quotes Michael Soskil, a head teacher and curriculum coach, as follows:

> Students are identifying problems in the world and working toward solving them, which is very important, of course, but they are also seeing the good they are doing and want to do more. Kids understand they are learning for a reason, and they connect with this idea for life. . . . It's neuroscience, in fact, where learning is stored in long-term memory when a child emotionally connects with the lesson being taught. (Douglas, 2015, p. 27)

Teachers can design projects with ELs that draw on the students' personal journeys from their country of origin, their family histories if they are children of immigrants who were born in the United States, or the cultural richness of their communities. This gives ELs the opportunity to build on their life experiences and culture in order to address real-world issues. It also allows students to transmit their background knowledge to others in the global learning community. The Buck Institute for Education (www .BIE.org) provides extensive resources and research on the use of project-based learning that is standards based and designed to maximize the creative potential of every student. They emphasize three elements essential to successful project-based learning.

The first element is in-depth inquiry, which requires that teachers work with students to develop the context and craft the questions for the project together. Teachers should design projects based on real-world challenges that encourage students to find concrete solutions and become engaged global citizens. The second element is voice and choice. This requires that students be involved in shaping the outcomes and determining the guidelines and agreements for student communication and collaboration throughout the term of the project, as well as respecting the needs of those from other cultures with whom the students may be collaborating. Finally, the attainment of 21st century skills is the third element and an essential feature of project-based learning. It is one of the end goals and not just a means to an end. To promote global awareness for students and stimulate discussion regarding global concerns visit the Global Oneness Project (http://www.globalonenessproject .org) for free multimedia resources and lesson plans.

Global PBL is closely aligned with the ISTE Standards for Promoting and Modeling Digital Citizenship (see sidebar).

UNDERSTANDING ELs

Capitalizing on Students' Funds of Knowledge

There has been a strong connection established between culture and language with many researchers suggesting that knowledge is obtained and shared from one's cultural environment (Moll, Amanti, Neff, & Gonzalez, 1992; Moll & Greenberg, 1990). More recently, Esteban-Guitart and Moll (2014) stated, "Children are active subjects who create special *funds of knowledge* and *identity* for themselves through their social actions and transactions" (p. 73; italics in original). Many of these social actions and transactions take place outside of school, within the cultural context of the children's home and community lives. We must keep in mind that ELs come to school with their own funds of knowledge and funds of identity originating from their home experiences.

This instructional model aligns seamlessly with the International Society for Technology in Education Standards for Teachers ISTE 4. a–d.

4. Promote and Model Digital Citizenship

   Teachers understand local and global societal issues and responsibilities in an evolving digital culture and exhibit legal and ethical behavior in their professional practices.

   a. Advocate, model, and teach safe, legal, and ethical use of digital information and technology, including respect for copyright, intellectual property, and the appropriate documentation of sources.

   b. Address the diverse needs of all learners by using learner-centered strategies providing equitable access to appropriate digital tools and resources.

   c. Promote and model digital etiquette and responsible social interactions related to the use of technology and information.

   d. Develop and model cultural understanding and global awareness by engaging with colleagues and students of other cultures using digital-age communication and collaboration tools.

SOURCE: International Society for Technology in Education (2016).

Children learn actively and construct knowledge outside of school as well, thus Moll et al. (1992) suggest that educators recognize and use funds of knowledge and identity to assist in student learning in school. We have to see students' "funds of knowledge" as "tool kits" (Esteban-Guitart & Moll, 2014, p. 73) created from the lived experiences students bring and build on in school settings. Suggestions for classroom implementation include the following:

- Inviting students to tell their personal stories (they may use digital tools to do so)
- Making sure students see their lives and experiences reflected in the curriculum as well as the digital resources offered to support the core curriculum
- Nurturing student expertise by publicly recognizing the out-of-school knowledge and skills students have
- Supporting students to make connections between their school and home experiences as they use technology tools
- Making text-to-self, text-to-world, and text-to-text connections (including digital texts) that allow for bridging home and school

Linton (2011) emphasized that curriculum must not only be standards based but also culturally significant for students to be able to relate to what is being taught. He further cautioned that

culturally relevant instruction is simply not about the heroes and holidays associated with a student's culture. Rather it represents the current culture lived by the student, all that it represents in terms of neighborhood, heritage, family, history, and sociopolitical issues. (p. 63)

What we teach and how we teach it cannot be disconnected from the broader cultural aspects of the local community. We must relate new learning directly to ELs' lived experiences so that they can better connect new learning to prior knowledge and also develop the new skills to become college and career ready.

CREATING A SENSE OF BELONGING AND ENGAGEMENT

Over a decade and a half ago, Osterman (2000) found that "students who feel that they belong have more positive attitudes about school, academic engagement and will invest more of themselves in the learning process" (p. 343). English learners, especially some subgroups such as recently arrived immigrant children, refugees, unaccompanied minors, and international adoptees, may find that they no longer belong to their home countries, yet they have not yet been fully accepted and integrated in their new communities. All teachers of ELs must develop advanced cultural proficiency skills that support their students' sense of belonging. "By being culturally competent, schools reinforce students' identities and create a sense of academic and physical safety for students and their families" (Tung et al., 2011, p. 9). Geneva Gay (2000) was among the first to discuss culturally responsive teaching (CRT), which suggests that teachers implement a curriculum that allows students to see themselves reflected in it and that they also foster cross-cultural communication skills among all students.

Blankstein (2007) bluntly stated that "if students are bored, they are also disengaged; for them, success in school is an uphill struggle" (p. 22). There are many more reasons why ELs might be prone to disengage from the learning process, such as not understanding what is being said and taught, limited opportunities for authentic meaning making, lack of prior knowledge about certain topics, and limited connections made to their own lives and lived experiences. The challenge we face is to create a learning environment in which ELs become and remain highly motivated and engaged to learn. What motivates ELs is as varied and complex as it might be for any other group of students, yet it is critical that we as teachers "move away from the deliverer of knowledge in a passive environment, to one where all learners are actively engaged in the construction of their knowledge" (Clapper, 2009, p. 1). Peer interaction, project-based learning, visual support, technology integration, choice assignments, and hands-on or kinesthetic learning were reported to be highly motivating for students (Wolpert-Gawron, 2012).

CONTENT AND LANGUAGE INTEGRATION

"Since language development is a complex, long-term process, students should have access to grade-level curriculum concurrently with language instruction" (Gottlieb & Ernst-Slavin, 2014, p. 25). Rigorous and culturally and linguistically responsive instruction designed for ELs can no longer focus on language or literacy skills in isolation. The most current understanding about ELs' needs requires that grade-level content and language instruction be integrated: as a result, ELs are taught in a way that they can begin to master the academic content, continue to expand their English language and literacy skills, become fully included members of the school community, and also feel supported in maintaining and enhancing their native language and literacy skills. The combination of these efforts truly leads to fostering global citizenship for all.

Technology has made it possible to conduct interdisciplinary projects within the same school community and beyond. An example of this is the

Global Water Sampling Project (http://www.k12science.org/curriculum/waterproj). Students from around the world test freshwater. Contributors assess the quality of the water samples and use the data collected to identify trends and relationships across the globe.

MAKE-IT-YOUR-OWN LESSON SEEDS

The following brief overviews provide a topic with "seed" ideas that we invite you to "grow" into a full lesson plan for your classroom.

Virtual Field Trip to State Capitol

In the following lesson seed, students will use their working knowledge and understanding of the concepts of citizenship, power, authority, and governance. Students will then use technology to locate the U.S. Capitol and other national buildings on Google Earth. Students will participate in a virtual field trip to Washington, D.C., and take notes during their experiential learning. Virtual field trips are less time consuming than a real trip and are budget friendly. They provide online access to many locations that your class may not get a chance to visit on their own. Students can explore many locations and discover extraordinary places just by using online virtual trip resources.

Virtual Field Trip to State Capitol

Grade Level: 3

Planning		Student Goals
Subject Area(s)		• **I can** describe the functions of state governments and define *capital* as the location of state and national government and *capitol* as the building in which government is located.
X	English language arts	
	Mathematics	• **I can** identify the nation's capital on a map and name the major national buildings and sites in Washington, D.C.
	Science	
X	Social studies	• **I can** use Google Earth to locate the U.S. Capitol and other national buildings. I can participate in a virtual tweet field trip using Twitter.
	Other:	
Language Skills		
X	Listening	**Activating Prior Knowledge**
X	Speaking	
X	Reading	Review the formation of the United States with an emphasis on citizenship, government, and economics. Using Google Earth, search places
X	Writing	
X	Viewing	

Resources and Supports	
X	Technology tools
X	Native language
X	Visuals, realia, manipulatives
X	Graphic organizers

Interaction-Grouping	
	Individual practice
	Pairs
X	Small group
	Whole group
X	Online collaboration

and navigate street views of Washington, D.C. Participate in a virtual field trip of the U.S. Capitol using the web resource Kids in the House (http://kids.clerk.house.gov) and Inside the White House (https://www.whitehouse.gov/about/inside-white-house/interactive-tour).

Engagement

Work in groups to research information on the web about the U.S. government and how bills become laws. Identify a problem in your community that might be resolved through legislation.

- Review, compare, and use notes to propose a new law for the community.
- Create a hashtag (#) to connect your group members to the virtual field trip.
- Tweet your experiences through pictures, videos, and links to the community.
- Respond to tweets with questions and comments.

Template adapted from WIDA Lesson Plan Share Space

https://www.wida.us/professionaldev/educatorresources/lessonPlan-shareSpace.aspx

Instagram Science Field Journal

The Internet has opened the doors for students to conduct real-world research. Students now have access to institutes of higher education, laboratories, museums, and classrooms around the globe. Understanding how to navigate this essential research tool is a requirement for all learners. However, we must also expose students to real-life scientific discovery and observation through field trips. ELs especially may have limited exposure to the research opportunities surrounding their local community.

According to the National Research Council (NRC) framework regarding science and engineering practice for planning and carrying out investigations,

students should have opportunities to plan and carry out several different kinds of investigations during their K–12 years. At all levels, they should engage in investigations that range from those structured by the teacher—in order to expose an issue or question that they would be unlikely to explore on their own (for example, measuring specific properties of materials)—to those that emerge from students' own questions. (National Research Council, 2012, p. 61)

(Continued)

(Continued)

In this lesson, students learn how to form their own guiding question for a science field trip, collect data during the field trip using Instagram, and then use the data to write a field journal entry.

Instagram Science Field Journal		
Grade Level: 12		

Planning		Student Goals
Subject Area(s)		<ul><li>**I can** collect and share data and conduct research while on a field trip.</li><li>**I can** write a field journal entry that includes a reflection about what I have discovered as well as questions about what I would like to investigate further.</li><li>**I can** use Instagram to make observations and share and collect data for my field journal.</li></ul>
X	English language arts	
	Mathematics	
X	Science	
	Social studies	
	Other:	
Language Skills		**Activating Prior Knowledge**
X	Listening	Generate a guiding question for the day based on the research you will be conducting.
X	Speaking	
X	Reading	Visit http://www2.epa.gov/students for ideas.
X	Writing	
X	Viewing	
Resources and Supports		**Engagement**
X	Technology tools	*Students:*
X	Native language	1. Create a list of things to find during the field trip, guided museum tour, or outdoor walking tour.
X	Visuals, realia, manipulatives	
X	Graphic organizers	2. Create a public Instagram account for school use. Be sure to get photo release consent.
Interaction-Grouping		3. Share your account name and unique hashtag with your teacher. Tag your teacher during the field trip when posting photos.
X	Individual practice	
	Pairs	
	Small group	4. Include a fact you learned or an insightful observation about each particular item from the list.
X	Whole group	
X	Online collaboration	5. Click the hashtag under any photo and see all the photos your classmates have posted for the field trip.

	Adapted from C. Tucker's lesson idea "Instagram Scavenger Hunt"; http://catlintucker.com/2013/02/instagram-scavenger-hunt.
Template adapted from WIDA Lesson Plan Share Space https://www.wida.us/professionaldev/educatorresources/lessonPlan-shareSpace.aspx	

CONSIDER THIS

ELs face a considerable challenge developing a bilingual, bicultural identity in a multilingual, multicultural U.S. context. Why is it critical to help ELs develop a global digital citizenship as well, and how can that be best achieved while honoring their complex cultural experiences?

DIGITAL AGE EXPLORER'S CORNER

Acquiring Life Skills Through a Blended Global Learning Community

The Sequoia Foundation, led by educational technology expert Patricia Machado, is helping high-need students learn English for specific purposes in eight neighborhoods in Rio de Janeiro, Brazil, through an innovative program called English Works. This unique blended learning experience combines face-to-face in-class instruction, online learning through Moodle, and live video conferencing for weekly conversation practice via Skype. Over 70 volunteers from around the world have been recruited to conduct Skype sessions with students every week. The goal of this interactive program is to provide communicative English and basic technology skills that will increase opportunities for low-income families. The program facilitates the acquisition of technology skills for the workplace and for social networking by encouraging students to interact online via Facebook, Twitter, and WhatsApp, as well as have an understanding of basic workplace productivity tools. They focus on building student confidence in order to enrich everyday life and find work in sectors such as IT, industry, finance, human resources, and tourism. Each course runs

(Continued)

(Continued)

for 14 weeks and is open to students ages 15 to 87 years old. They have over 4,000 students and receive 6,000 applicants a year (see http://sqafoundation.org/sqahome/investing-for-brazil/english-works).

CHAPTER SUMMARY

Teaching digital citizenship explicitly is essential for safe and effective online collaboration.

Incorporating social media into lesson plans expands opportunities for ELs to interact authentically in the target language and get content area support.

Project-based learning encourages critical thinking and creativity through authentic problem solving.

Virtual field trips help to bring topics to life and enrich academic background knowledge while helping ELs expand their worldview.

Global project-based learning allows ELs to tap into their cultural experiences in order to address real-world issues.

The Internet allows ELs to conduct real-world research, collaborate with other communities of learners, and develop 21st century skills.

PLN QUESTIONS

1. How might you integrate global awareness into cross-curricular lessons that address both language and content development?

2. How can social networking tools engage ELs in authentic content and language learning?

3. Why is it important to use EL students' funds of knowledge to make new learning relevant and meaningful?

4. How can we engage parents of ELs to teach digital citizenship when a language barrier or lack of technology skills exists?

5. Describe a project-based learning activity that you have used or would like to use with your students. How would you adapt the activity for ELs?

8 Critical Thinking and Assessment

The major part of this story relates to the power of directed teaching, enhancing what happens next (through feedback and monitoring) to inform the teacher about the success or failure of their teaching, and to provide a method to evaluate the relative efficacy of different influences that teachers use. (John Hattie, 2009, p. 6)

OVERVIEW

This chapter explores the way that a digital age learning environment can help teachers transform traditional assessment to better inform instruction and more accurately reflect the academic progress of English learners. The digital age learning environment shifts the culture of preparing students for standardized assessments to preparing assessments based on learning experiences within the classroom. Hattie (2009) stated, "The teacher provides supportive feedback and helps students to learn by acknowledging and using the student's prior knowledge and experiences, and monitoring to check if students know what is being taught, what is to be learnt, or what is to be produced" (p. 6). The digital age learning environment ensures that ELs have authentic learning experiences, digital tools that promote student learning, and multiple ways to show their success in the classroom. This chapter will bring about a change in the way teachers view and create assessments for ELs. Teachers will create alternative assessments featuring technology tools so that English learners have more ways to experience success.

DIGITAL AGE LEARNING EXPERIENCE

Creating Alternative Assessments

When teachers design classroom assessments, they intend to measure the amount of knowledge students have learned. When teachers create alternative assessments featuring technology tools, they intend to measure the student's ability to perform a task based on a learning outcome. Teachers that encourage a digital age learning environment "think out of the box" when creating assessments that show what students have accomplished. These assessments may include online collaboration, project-based learning, and multimedia presentations. The collaboration within a digital age classroom promotes a culture of critical thinking, inquiry, and discovery. Shared learning gives students an opportunity to engage in discussion and take responsibility for their own learning, thus becoming critical thinkers (Totten, Sills, Digby, & Russ, 1991). When the right technology tool is integrated into a content-rich lesson, it provides multisensory access to that content, facilitating comprehension and allowing ELs to participate more effectively in academic discourse. Technology tools can be used to scaffold activities that may otherwise be difficult for ELs to understand. In addition, using technology tools to deliver content and assess student performance enhances traditional methods of delivery that are largely text based. This opens up the door to critical thinking by lowering the language barrier and channeling the instructional focus to academic content.

Creating alternative or authentic assessments that feature technology tools may take more time and effort to create, but the value for ELs is significant. Alternative assessments afford ELs opportunities to develop ideas and freely participate in the classroom. The focus of assessments is on student performance and the process and quality of the student's work. For example, teachers can use personal response systems (clickers) or an online polling application that allows for real-time communication and collaboration between the teacher and students. Applications, such as Kahoot!, Socrative, or Plickers, provide insight into levels of understanding among students and allow teachers to inform their instruction in ways that meet the needs of English learners. Students use their mobile device (or a paper response card for Plickers) to answer yes/no or multiple-choice questions that are transmitted immediately to the teacher's device. By using this approach, participation becomes inclusive for all levels of English learners by lowering the affective variables that can negatively influence motivation, self-confidence, and anxiety within the classroom (Krashen, 2014). Personal response clickers and opportunities to survey the class ensure that each student has a voice. Instead of relying on teacher-directed activities and formal assessments, teachers focus on instructional time that provides fun, quick, and easy access to evaluate and inform their instruction and identify the support needed for struggling learners.

When teachers implement alternative assessments featuring technology tools, student engagement increases and teachers can gain access to their students' progress instantaneously. The virtual bulletin board Padlet offers students a place to immediately share their thoughts or ideas with the class. Students can post text, images, links, or videos on the virtual wall to answer open-ended questions regarding a book review, extend discussions, share their viewpoints, or use ExitTicket (exittix.com) to demonstrate what they've learned.

Many teachers are incorporating digital portfolios into their classrooms. Digital portfolios allow for more self-directed learning and collaboration among teachers, students, and parents. Digital portfolios or e-portfolios enable teachers to capture and share their students' academic and creative development, provide opportunities for student reflection, and gather authentic information to improve students' learning process and progress.

Teachers can also gather data to inform instruction, provide additional support, and notify parents. An online behavioral management tool such as ClassDojo can assess and monitor student behaviors and allow teachers to share information with parents in an online communication platform.

Many English learners struggle with demonstrating their learning through traditional methods. For ELs, proficiency in reading and writing limits their participation within the classroom. By using alternative assessments featuring technology tools, teachers can monitor and gauge the skills students have developed based on their performance. For instance, a blog can be used to encourage ELs to read and write in a positive forum that encourages participation and motivation. Blogs can be used for assessment purposes in several ways. By posing questions and discussions among students, ELs can share their thoughts and ideas without the intimidation of having to speak in front of a class. Teachers can use blogs to allow students to respond to or reflect on a specific lesson or topic. When teachers maintain a professional website or when they create a class website, they make their teaching visible and their expectations transparent. These websites may or may not require a special log-in protocol, depending on the level of privacy you wish to establish. If ELs are able to access information after they leave school, it may work as an extension to the learning that took place in class as well as serve as a link between home and school.

The 21st century classroom teacher can adopt new ways to use assessments to diagnose and modify instruction for English learners. Traditional and standardized assessments do not usually reflect the skills and abilities

This instructional model aligns seamlessly with the International Society for Technology in Education Standards for Teachers ISTE 2. a–d.

2. Design and Develop Digital Age Learning Experiences and Assessments

   Teachers design, develop, and evaluate authentic learning experiences and assessments incorporating contemporary tools and resources to maximize content learning in context and to develop the knowledge, skills, and attitudes identified in the ISTE Student Standards.

   a. Design or adapt relevant learning experiences that incorporate digital tools and resources to promote student learning and creativity.

   b. Develop technology-enriched learning environments that enable all students to pursue their individual curiosities and become active participants in setting their own educational goals, managing their own learning, and assessing their own progress.

   c. Customize and personalize learning activities to address students' diverse learning styles, working strategies, and abilities using digital tools and resources.

   d. Provide students with multiple and varied formative and summative assessments aligned with content and technology standards, and use resulting data to inform learning and teaching.

SOURCE: International Society for Technology in Education (2016).

of ELs. Using technology to create alternative assessments provides teachers with frequent opportunities to examine, refine, and redirect their instruction in ways that can support language development for ELs. Technology can support measuring performance that cannot be assessed with conventional testing formats, providing our education system with opportunities to design, develop, and validate new and more effective assessment materials. Building this capacity can be accelerated through knowledge exchange, collaboration, and better alignment between educators (practitioners) and the experts (Office of Educational Technology, n.d.).

UNDERSTANDING ELs

Assessment Practices and ELs

Margo Gottlieb (2016) presents a unique framework that describes assessment for ELs from three perspectives.

1. *Assessment as learning* suggests that English learners can meaningfully contribute to the assessment process. Through self-assessment and reflection, ELs develop agency and become more self-directed, independent learners, who can do the following:

   a. Learn to set their own goals

   b. Monitor and reflect on their progress

    c. Make choices of assessment task projects when offered

    d. Develop and maintain a student portfolio

    e. Participate in the assessment process in many other ways

2. *Assessment for learning* refers to the process that both classroom teachers and ELD/ESL specialists may employ on a regular basis. Teachers collect evidence of the learning targets their students have mastered, those they are in the process of mastering, and those they have yet to attain. Assessment for learning is primarily formative in nature, and as such, it helps inform instruction and offer feedback to students. Based on the formative assessment data collected, teachers may make adjustments to their teaching immediately or plan on reteaching a given skill or concept the following class session. Heritage (2011) notes that "teacher feedback is most beneficial when it assists students to understand their current learning status and provides hints, suggestions, or cues for them to act on. It is this, rather than offering general praise or total solutions, that enables students to assume a degree of responsibility for their learning" (p. 18).

3. *Assessment of learning* refers to processes that yield summative assessment data, including standardized testing. Nontraditional performance-based or project-based assessments encourage learners to demonstrate what they have learned in creative ways, often allowing for the use of multiple modalities rather than responding to a traditional pencil and paper test.

Among many others, Sandberg and Reschly (2011) acknowledge the challenges teachers face when creating curriculum-based measurements and assessing ELs. Although differentiating instruction for ELs is becoming widely accepted and practiced, when it comes to assessment, teachers might continue to assign identical projects and give identical quizzes and tests. Teachers must collaborate not only to differentiate instruction but to design differentiated assessment tools as well. Honigsfeld and Dove (2010, 2015) suggest that coassessment is a crucial yet often overlooked element of the collaborative instructional cycle that also includes coplanning, codelivering instruction, and refection on one's teaching. Technology-based tools such as Google Forms are ideal for progress monitoring and sharing information about ELs. When collaborating, teachers have editing rights to the (codeveloped) form and can have access to the data collected by each team member. Collaborative data collection and analysis help set consistent goals for ELs as well as support a more integrated approach to serving ELs.

Willner, Rivera, and Acosta (2009) suggest what the entire school faculty should learn about accommodating ELs during formal assessments. According to Willner et al. (2009), there are five key components to keep in mind:

- Focus on teaching grade-appropriate content to ELs
- Provide accommodations that support ELs' linguistic needs
- Assign accommodations based on individual student needs
- Use a team approach when making accommodation decisions
- Provide the opportunity to use the accommodations before the test

Another approach is to design alternative assessments that allow students to demonstrate what they have learned and what they can do without the linguistic burden traditional assessments place on ELs. Selecting performance-based, project-based, or other types of authentic assessment tools serve ELs well because they provide "direct insights on the students' progress and accomplishments" (Lenski, Ehlers-Zavala, Daniel, & Sun-Irminger, 2006, p. 28).

ELs may either be underrepresented or overrepresented in special educational services but tend to be underrepresented in specially designed programs for gifted and talented students. One reason for these patterns is the limitations presented by tools and measures educators use during the identification process. ELs with exceptional needs (be it a learning disability, a language learning disorder, or giftedness) have to be fully supported to reach their full potential academically, linguistically, and socially. A critical approach to the teaching and assessment of these youngsters is to maximize their ability and their opportunity to master and express knowledge of the target content.

We firmly believe in and advocate for recognizing that limited English fluency does not indicate a lack of academic potential. Just the contrary, with the right amount and types of supports and scaffolds, all ELs can make reasonable progressions and succeed in and out of school.

MAKE-IT-YOUR-OWN LESSON SEEDS

The following brief overviews provide a topic with "seed" ideas that we invite you to "grow" into a full lesson plan for your classroom.

Patterns

In the following lesson seed, students will learn how to identify and group shapes and patterns by attributes, such as size, color, and shape. Students will then use technology to extend patterns by choosing the correct object. Students will use digital media, photos, and visuals in creating and completing their own patterns.

Patterns	
Grade Level: Kindergarten	

Planning	Student Goals
	• **I can** identify and group shapes such as squares, triangles, rectangles, and circles in English and Spanish.

Planning / **Student Goals**

Subject Area(s)	
X	English language arts
	Mathematics
	Science
	Social studies
X	Other: Art

Student Goals

- **I can** identify and group shapes such as squares, triangles, rectangles, and circles in English and Spanish.
- **I can** describe the attributes of the objects by size, color, and shape.
- **I can** use a drawing software program to complete a shapes pattern created by the teacher. I can then create my own pattern for my classmates to solve.

Language Skills	
X	Listening
X	Speaking
X	Reading
X	Writing
X	Viewing

Activating Prior Knowledge

Brainstorm with the class different types of shapes and their attributes.

Identify the vocabulary and name the shapes pictured on the SMART Board. Create a pattern on the SMART Board of two shapes. Guess the shape to complete the pattern.

Resources and Supports	
X	Technology tools
X	Native language
X	Visuals, realia, manipulatives
X	Graphic organizers

Engagement

- Work in pairs to identify shape patterns created by the teacher using Tux Paint.
- Work together to create a simple two-shape pattern on Tux Paint. Use the Tux Paint drawing tools and stamps.
- Name the patterns and shapes in English and/or Spanish using SMART Response System clickers.

Interaction-Grouping	
	Individual practice
X	Pairs
	Small group
	Whole group
X	Online collaboration

Template adapted from WIDA Lesson Plan Share Space

https://www.wida.us/professionaldev/educatorresources/lessonPlan-shareSpace.aspx

(Continued)

(Continued)

Mystery Skype

"Mystery Skype" lessons are interactive and engaging videoconferences. Two classrooms of students connect via Skype or Google Hangouts without knowing each other's location. Students must ask geography questions in order to identify the "mystery" location of the other class. The first class to identify the location of the other class wins. This activity requires an organized team effort, critical thinking, and fact recall, as well as research and map skills. It is a problem-solving activity that provides immediate feedback in an authentic context for ELs to practice listening and speaking.

Mystery Skype		Student Goals
Grade Level: 8		
Planning		• **I can** use map skills to locate places in the United States. I can recall facts about the United States to help identify a "mystery classroom."
Subject Area(s)		• **I can** think critically to construct, ask, and answer questions about the United States and regions within it to help uncover a mystery classroom's location.
X	English language arts	• **I can** collaborate with other students virtually via Skype or Google Hangouts and use Google Maps to help solve clues about the mystery classroom's location.
	Mathematics	
	Science	
X	Social studies	
	Other:	
Language Skills		**Activating Prior Knowledge**
X	Listening	Using Google Earth, review the geographic locations in the United States that have been introduced, including names of states, cities, capitals, and counties.
X	Speaking	
X	Reading	
X	Writing	Review vocabulary: *longitude*, *latitude*, and *cardinal directions*.
X	Viewing	
Resources and Supports		Model question format for the Mystery Skype activity. Prepare a set of 20 questions to ask and 5–10 clues to provide to the other class.
X	Technology tools	
X	Native language	For example: Are you east of the Mississippi?
X	Visuals, realia, manipulatives	
X	Graphic organizers	(Assign specific roles to students prior to the call, such as greeters, inquirers, responders, clue trackers, brainstormers, runners, videographers, problem solvers.)
Interaction-Grouping		
	Individual practice	
	Pairs	
	Small group	
X	Whole group	
X	Online collaboration	

Engagement

- To find other teachers who would like to connect with your classroom for a Mystery Skype session visit https://mysterystate.wikispaces.com.
- Connect with another classroom and set a day and time to meet.
- Rehearse with your class before the actual call.
- During the call try to guess each other's location by asking the prepared questions and developing new ones as needed. Keep track of responses and use your content knowledge, Google Maps, and other classroom resources to solve the mystery.

(The students lead the conversation as the teacher assesses and facilitates the process.)

Template adapted from WIDA Lesson Plan Share Space

https://www.wida.us/professionaldev/educatorresources/lessonPlan-shareSpace.aspx

CONSIDER THIS

In a recent *Educational Leadership* article, Diane Staehr Fenner (2016) suggests that her work with ELs is based in an advocacy framework. She introduces the concept of *scaffolded advocacy*, which refers to "providing just the right amount of advocacy on the basis of students' strengths and needs (para. 4). What does scaffolded advocacy mean to you in light of the discussion of assessment practices in this chapter? What is the role of technology to ensure scaffolded advocacy?

DIGITAL AGE EXPLORER'S CORNER

Data Collection and Student Management Systems for ELs

Many school districts use a web-based software program specifically designed for educators of ELs to monitor, track, and support English learners. Ellevation allows teachers of ELs to review proficiency levels and accommodations and monitor current, reclassified, and exited students. Teachers can filter and view data at the district, grade,

(Continued)

(Continued)

classroom, and school levels to easily view trends and group students. To personalize instruction for English learners, teachers use Ellevation to get a sharp understanding of each student's strengths and challenges, and work closely with colleagues to develop plans and coordinate instruction for coteaching classrooms.

Many student management systems offer quick and easy access to store and track student and classroom data. It is important for districts to find the right solution that focuses on making data-driven decisions that personalize learning, increase communication and equip teachers, students, and parents with the latest technology tools.

CHAPTER SUMMARY

A digital age learning environment can help teachers transform traditional assessment to better inform instruction and more accurately reflect the academic progress of English learners.

ELs are provided authentic learning experiences, digital tools that promote student learning, and multiple ways to show their success in the classroom.

Alternative assessments featuring technology tools measure the student's ability to perform a task based on a learning outcome.

Teachers can use personal response systems (clickers) or an online polling application that allows for real-time communication and collaboration between the teacher and students.

Online behavioral management tools can assess and monitor student behaviors and allow teachers to share information with parents in an online communication platform.

Teachers can use blogs to allow students to respond to or reflect on a specific lesson or topic.

Technology can support measuring performance that cannot be assessed with conventional testing formats, providing our education system with opportunities to design, develop, and validate new and more effective assessment materials.

PLN QUESTIONS

1. In what ways do you measure digital literacy in your classroom?

2. How can alternative assessments featuring technology tools identify student success in the classroom?

3. How can alternative assessments featuring technology tools help teachers identify students that need more assistance?

4. Examine traditional and standardized assessments and describe the advantages and disadvantages for ELs.

5. How do alternative assessments featuring technology tools lower the affective variables that can negatively influence motivation, self-confidence, and anxiety within the classroom for ELs?

9 **Parting Thoughts**

The digital revolution has changed the composition of work and posed a challenge for education no less profound than the challenge posed to society by the change from horses to automobiles over 100 years ago. (Edwards, 2014, p. 18)

IMPLEMENTING CHANGE BY BUILDING TRUST

In order to truly initiate any change, it is important to involve all stakeholders. Administrators, teachers, parents, students, and community members all have a part to play in making a digital age transition a reality. A good starting point is to create a professional learning network that includes a variety of stakeholders who are willing to explore new ideas together. This book can be used as a tool for discussion and experimentation. Teachers can expand on the lesson seeds provided, and the PLN questions at the end of each chapter can spark conversation. Most importantly, working together toward these goals will help to develop and build trust in the transition process and provide the foundation for real change.

In *The Speed of Trust*, Stephen Covey (2008) describes the benefits of building trust to improve a business organization's performance. This same philosophy is necessary for educational institutions in order to create a digital age environment for ELs. In a high-trust environment, students are more likely to experiment with new ideas, take risks, be innovative, and complete tasks more efficiently. Most ELs are also more likely to participate with enthusiasm in partnered and group activities.

Implementing change supports the International Society for Technology in Education Standards for Teachers ISTE 5. a–d:

5. Engage in Professional Growth and Leadership

   Teachers continuously improve their professional practice, model lifelong learning , and exhibit leadership in their school and professional community by promoting and demonstrating the effective use of digital tools and resources.

   a. Participate in local and global learning communities to explore creative applications of technology to improve student learning.

   b. Exhibit leadership by demonstrating a vision of technology infusion, participating in shared decision making and community building, and developing the leadership and technology skills of others.

   c. Evaluate and reflect on current research and professional practice on a regular basis to make effective use of existing and emerging digital tools and resources in support of student learning.

   d. Contribute to the effectiveness, vitality, and self-renewal of the teaching profession and of their school and community.

SOURCE: International Society for Technology in Education (2016).

Ultimately, a trusting environment accelerates student growth and helps to develop self-directed, independent learners. For ELs, who are oftentimes still adjusting to a new cultural environment, a feeling of safety and trust in the classroom is essential to learning. Furthermore, ELs who feel safe in the classroom will be more likely to tolerate ambiguity and to experiment with the use of English while collaborating with peers, thereby accelerating the language learning process.

How can teachers build trust and promote collaboration within the ELD/ESL classroom? The digital tools that are now available to teachers allow them to design learning tasks and manage classroom workflow so that students are empowered to work independently and collaboratively. When teachers act as curators of information, they design projects that set groups of students on a learning journey. The journey includes the use of technology to research, problem solve, and create multimedia projects to demonstrate mastery of a topic together. This type of project-based learning dispels the common myth that students who use technology in the classroom work in isolation with their face buried in a screen, interacting with no one. Instead, the classroom is transformed into a laboratory for learning that uses all five language skills—listening, speaking, reading, writing, and viewing—while emphasizing the 5 C's for 21st century ELs: critical thinking, communication, collaboration, creativity, and culture.

DIGITAL AGE TEACHING FOR ENGLISH LEARNERS (DATELs)

We hope that this book has provided a starting point for teachers and administrators to reflect on current practices and take first steps toward creating a digital age learning environment for a new generation of English learners. The strategies, tools, and lesson seeds provided will help to transform current classroom practices into more student-centered, project-based environments that are infused with useful technology that enriches and supports learning. Figure 9.1 identifies the key features of DATELs and illustrates how a digital age learning environment for ELs will do the following:

- Increase social interaction and engagement
- Provide authentic communication and contextually rich language practice
- Reduce the affective filter so that more learning can occur
- Support scaffolded instruction through digital tools and media
- Incorporate the five language skills (listening, speaking, reading, writing, and viewing)
- Emphasize the 5 C's for 21st century ELs (critical thinking, communication, collaboration, creativity, and culture)

Figure 9.1   D.A.T.E.L.s

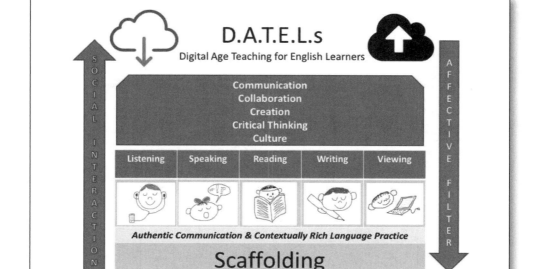

Appendix A

Technology Tools and Resources

Chapter 2	audioBoom	DocScan	eBackpack	LiveBinders	Symbaloo
	Canvas	Dropbox	eSpark	Notability	Tagxedo
	Desire2Learn	Edublogs	Evernote	Qrafter	Wordle
Chapter 3	Bitsboard	Kid in Story	News-O-matic	See.Touch.Learn	Word Mover
	BrainPOP	LearnZillion	Popplet	Shakespeare In Bits	WriteAbout
	iTunes Podcasts	Newsela	Rewordify	Tellagami	Voice Record Pro
Chapter 4	Book Creator	Garage Band	Google Slides	Keynote	Puppet Pals
	Comic Life	Glogster	iBook Author	PowToon	SoundCloud
	ePub Bud	Google Sites	iMovie	Prezi	Weebly
Chapter 5	Zaption	Educreations	Khan Academy	PBS Media	ShowMe
	Camtasia	Explain Everything	Videolicious	Screencast-O-Matic	TED-Ed
	EDpuzzle	Flipped Learning Network	Nearpod	ScreenChomp	YouTube

(Continued)

(Continued)

Chapter 6	Artsonia	FieldTripZoom	Google Drive	iTunes U	Skype
	Blendspace	Google Art Project	Google Hangouts	Moodle	Tackk
	FaceTime	Google Classroom	Graphite	Polycom	Wikispaces
Chapter 7	Discovery Ed	Google Earth	ISTE PLN	School Leadership 2.0	Twitter
	Edmodo	Google Plus	Ning	Schoology	Global Water Sampling Project
	Global Oneness Project	Instagram	Pinterest	The Global Classroom Project	VoiceThread K–12
Chapter 8	ClassDojo	Flubaroo	JogNog	Poll Everywhere	SMART Response
	Cramberry	Google Forms	Mystery Skype	Quizlet	Socrative
	ExitTicket	Kahoot!	Plickers	Raz-Kids	Three Ring

Appendix B

ELD/ESL Methodology Resources

- APPitic Educational Website: www.facebook.com/Appitic/timeline
- Avanzamos Conectados: www.commonsensemedia.org/espanol/blog/avanzamos-conectados
- Breaking News English: www.breakingnewsenglish.com
- Buck Institute for Education: bie.org
- Center for Applied Linguistics (CAL): www.cal.org
- Center on English Learning & Achievement: www.albany.edu/cela
- Colorín Colorado: www.colorincolorado.org
- Common Sense Media: www.commonsensemedia.org
- DocsTeach: teachinghistory.org/digital-classroom/tech-for-teachers/24268
- EdSurge: www.edsurge.com
- Educational Resources Information Center (ERIC) on English Language Learners: eric.ed.gov/?q=English+Language+Learners
- Education Technology and Mobile Learning: www.educatorstechnology.com
- #ELLCHAT: www.facebook.com/ELLCHAT-105656129477631
- EngageNY: www.engageny.org
- ESL Café: www.eslcafe.com
- ESL Connect: www.eslconnect.com/links.html
- ESL Techies: esltechies.com
- Everything ESL: www.everythingesl.net

- 4Teachers: www.4teachers.org
- GCF Learn Free: www.gcflearnfree.org
- International Literacy Association: www.literacyworldwide.org
- ISTE: www.iste.org
- Larry Ferlazzo: larryferlazzo.edublogs.org
- Literacy Center Education Network: www.literacycenter.net
- Mind/Shift: ww2.kqed.org/mindshift
- National Association of Bilingual Education (NABE): www.nabe.org
- National Clearinghouse for English Language Acquisition (NCELA): www.ncela.ed.gov
- New York Times Learning Network: learning.blogs.nytimes.com
- Northeast and Islands Regional Educational Laboratory: www.relnei.org
- OWL Purdue Online Writing Lab: owl.english.purdue.edu/owl/section/5/24
- Partnership for 21st Century Learning: www.P21.org
- Project Gutenberg: www.gutenberg.org
- Readwritethink: www.readwritethink.org
- RITELL—Resources for Teachers: www.ritell.org/Default.aspx?pageId=1800810
- Stanford University's Understanding Language Program: ell.stanford.edu
- Teachers of English to Speakers of Other Languages (TESOL): www.tesol.org
- Teaching Channel: www.teachingchannel.org
- United States Department of Education: www.ed.gov
- Varsity Tutors: www.varsitytutors.com/englishteacher/esl.html
- WestEd: www.wested.org

References

Applebee, A. N., Langer, J. A., Nystrand, M., & Gamoran, A. (2003). Student performance in middle and high school English discussion-based approaches to developing understanding: Classroom instruction and student performance in middle and high school English. *American Educational Research Journal, 40,* 685–730. doi:10.3102/00028312040003685

Bambrick-Santoyo, P. A., Settles, A., & Worrell, J. (2013). *Great habits, great readers: A practical guide to K–4 reading in light of the Common Core.* San Francisco: Jossey-Bass.

Beck, I. L., McKeown, M. G., & Kucan, L. (2013). *Bringing words to life: Robust vocabulary instruction* (2nd ed.). New York: Guilford.

Bergmann, J., & Sams, A. (2012). *Flip your classroom: Reach every student in every class every day.* Washington, DC: ISTE.

Blankstein, A. M. (2007). Terms of engagement: When failure is not an option. In A. M. Blankstein, R. W. Cole, & P. D. Houston (Eds.), *Engaging every learner* (pp. 1–28). Thousand Oaks, CA: Corwin.

Boyd, M. P., & Galda, L. (2011). *Real talk in elementary classrooms: Effective oral language practice.* New York: Guilford.

Brennan, W. (2013). *School principals and virtual learning: A catalyst to personal and organizational learning.* Unpublished doctoral dissertation, Fordham University, New York. Retrieved from http://www.brennanlearning.com.

Cazden, C. B. (2001). *Classroom discourse: The language of teaching and learning* (2nd ed.). Portsmouth, NH: Heinemann.

Clapper, T. C. (2009). Moving away from teaching and becoming a facilitator of learning. *PAILAL, 2*(2). Retrieved from http://www.academia.edu/1180001/Moving_away_from_teaching_and_becoming_a_facilitator_of_learning.

Covey, S. (2008). *The speed of trust: The one thing that changes everything.* New York: Simon & Schuster.

Covili, J. (2012). *Going Google: Powerful tools for 21st century learning.* Thousand Oaks, CA: Corwin.

Cullen, R., Kullman, J., & Wild, C. (2013). Online collaborative learning on an ESL teacher education programme. *ELT Journal, 67*(4), 425–434.

Dorfman, L. R., & Cappelli, R. (2007). *Mentor texts: Teaching writing through children's literature, K–6.* Portland, ME: Stenhouse.

Douglas, T. (2015, July). Cultural Connections: Students gain real-life insights with global PBL. *Entrsekt*, 24–31.

Dove, M. G., Honigsfeld, A., & Cohan, A. (2014). *Beyond core expectations: A school-wide framework for serving the not-so-common learner.* Thousand Oaks, CA: Corwin.

Echevarria, J., Vogt, M. E., & Short, D. (2012). *Making content comprehensible for English learners: The SIOP model* (4th ed.). Boston: Pearson.

Edwards, M. A. (2014). *Every child, every day: A digital conversion model for student achievement.* Boston: Pearson,

Esteban-Guitart, M., & Moll, L. C. (2014). Lived experience, funds of identity and education. *Culture & Psychology, 20,* 70–81. doi:10.1177/1354067X13515940

Fang, Z. (2012). Approaches to developing content area literacies: A synthesis and a critique. *Journal of Adolescent & Adult Literacy, 56,* 103–107. doi:10.1002/JAAL.00110

Fisher, D., & Frey, N. (2008). *Better learning through structured teaching: A framework for the gradual release of responsibility.* Alexandria, VA: ASCD.

Fisher, D., & Frey, N. (2009). *Background knowledge: The missing piece of the comprehension puzzle.* Portsmouth, NH: Heinemann.

García, O. (2009). *Bilingual education in the 21st century: A global perspective.* New York: Blackwell/Wiley.

García, O., & Li, W. (2014). *Translanguaging: Language, bilingualism, and education.* New York: Palgrave Macmillan.

Gay, G. (2000). *Culturally responsive teaching: Theory, research, and practice.* New York: Teachers College Press.

Goldenberg, C. N. (1992). *Instructional conversations and their classroom application* (Educational Practice Report 2). Santa Cruz, CA: National Center for Research on Diversity and Second Language Learning, University of California.

Goldenberg, C. N. (2008). Teaching English language learners: What the research does—and does not—say. *American Educator, 32*(2), 8–23, 42–44. Retrieved from http://www.aft.org/pdfs/americaneducator/summer2008/goldenberg.pdf.

Gottlieb, M. (2016). *Assessing English language learners: Bridges to educational equity.* Thousand Oaks, CA: Corwin.

Gottlieb, M., & Ernst-Slavin, G. (2014). *Academic language in diverse classrooms: Definitions and contexts.* Thousand Oaks, CA: Corwin.

Hattie, J. (2009). *Visible learning: A synthesis of over 800 meta-analyses relating to achievement.* New York: Routledge.

Hattie, J. (2012). *Visible learning for teachers: Maximizing impact on learning.* New York: Routledge.

Hattie, J., & Yates, G. (2014). *Visible learning and the science of how we learn.* New York: Routledge.

Heritage, M. (2011, Spring). Formative assessment: An enabler of learning. *Better: Evidence-Based Education*, 18–19. Retrieved from http://www.amplify.com/assets/regional/Heritage_FA.pdf.

Hobbs, R. (2011). *Digital and media literacy: Connecting culture and classroom.* Thousand Oaks, CA: Corwin.

Holtgraves, T. M. (2002). *Language as social action: Social psychology and language use.* Mahwah, NJ: Lawrence Erlbaum.

Honigsfeld, A., & Dove, M. G. (2010). *Collaboration and co-teaching: Strategies for English learners.* Thousand Oaks, CA: Corwin.

Honigsfeld, A., & Dove, M. G. (2015). *Collaboration and co-teaching: A leader's guide.* Thousand Oaks, CA: Corwin.

International Society for Technology in Education Teacher and Student Standards. (2016). *ISTE standards for students.* Retrieved from http://www.iste.org/standards/ISTE-standards/standards-for-students.

Johnson, D. W., & Johnson, R. (1999). *Learning together and alone: Cooperative, competitive, and individualistic learning* (5th ed.). Boston: Allyn & Bacon.

Krashen, S. (2014). *Stephen Krashen's theory of second language acquisition.* Retrieved from http://sk.com.br/sk-krash.html.

Lenski, S. D., Ehlers-Zavala, F., Daniel, M., & Sun-Irminger, X. (2006). Assessing English-language learners in mainstream classrooms. *The Reading Teacher, 60*(1), 24–34.

Linton, C. (2011). *Equity 101: The equity framework.* Thousand Oaks, CA: Corwin.

Lundy-Ponce, G. (2010). *Migrant students: What we need to know to help them succeed.* Retrieved from http://www.colorincolorado.org/article/migrant-students-what-we-need-know-help-them-succeed.

Marzano, R. J. (2004). *Building background knowledge for academic achievement: Research on what works in schools.* Alexandria, VA: ASCD.

McGroarty, M. (1993). Cooperative learning and second language acquisition. In D. D. Holt (Ed.), *Cooperative learning: A response to linguistic and cultural diversity* (pp. 19–46). Washington, DC: Delta Systems and Center for Applied Linguistics.

Michaels, S., O'Connor, M. C., Hall, M. W. (with Resnick, L. B.). (2010). *Accountable talk: Classroom conversation that works* (Version 3.1). Pittsburgh, PA: University of Pittsburgh.

Moll, L. C. (1992). Bilingual classroom studies and community analysis: Some recent trends. *Educational Researcher, 21*(2), 20–24.

Moll, L. C., Amanti, C., Neff, D., & Gonzalez, N. (1992). Funds of knowledge for teaching: Using a qualitative approach to connect homes and classrooms. *Theory Into Practice, 21*, 132–141.

Moll, L. C., & Greenberg, J. (1990). Creating zones of possibilities: Combining social contexts for instruction. In L. C. Moll (Ed.), *Vygotsky and education* (pp. 319–348). Cambridge, UK: Cambridge University Press.

Moss, C. M., & Brookhart, S. M. (2012). *Learning targets: Helping students aim for understanding in today's lesson.* Alexandria, VA: ASCD.

National Council of Teachers of English. (1996). *Standards for the English language arts.* Retrieved from https://secure.ncte.org/store/standards-for-the-english-language-arts.

National Education Association (NEA). (n.d.). *Preparing 21st century students for a global society. An educator's guide to the 'four C's'.* Retrieved from http://www.nea.org/assets/docs/A-Guide-to-Four-Cs.pdf.

National Institute of Child Health and Human Development (NICHHD). (2000). *Report of the National Reading Panel. Teaching children to read: An evidence-based assessment of the scientific research literature on reading and its implications for reading instruction: Reports of the subgroups* (NIH Publication No. 00-4754). Washington, DC: U.S. Government Printing Office.

National Research Council. (2012). *A framework for K–12 science education: Practices, crosscutting concepts, and core ideas.* Committee on a Conceptual Framework for New K–12 Science Education Standards. Board on Science Education, Division of Behavioral and Social Sciences and Education. Washington, DC: The National Academies Press. Retrieved from: http://www.nap.edu/read/13165/chapter/7#61.

New York State Education Department. (2011). *Guidelines for educating limited English proficient students with interrupted formal education (LEP/ELL/SIFES).* Retrieved from http://www.p12.nysed.gov/biling/docs/NYSEDSIFEGuide lines.pdf.

November, A. C. (2012). *Who owns the learning? Preparing students for success in the digital age.* Bloomington, IN: Solution Tree.

Office of Educational Technology. (n.d.). *Assessment: Measure what matters.* Retrieved from http://tech.ed.gov/netp/assessment-measure-what-matters.

O'Hara, S., Zwiers, J., & Pritchard, R. (2013). *Framing the development of complex language and literacy.* Retrieved from http://aldnetwork.org/sites/default/files/pictures/aldn_brief_2013.pdf.

Osterman, K. (2000). Students' need for belongingness in the school community. *Review of Educational Research, 70*(3), 323–367.

Parker, W. C. (2006). Public discourses in schools: Purposes, problems, possibilities. *Educational Researcher, 35*(8), 11–18. doi:10.3102/0013189X035008011

Pearson, P. D., & Gallagher, G. (1983). The gradual release of responsibility model of instruction. *Contemporary Education Psychology, 8,* 112–123.

Prensky, M. (2010). *Teaching digital natives: Partnering for real learning.* Thousand Oaks, CA: Corwin.

Purcell, K., Buchanan, J., & Friedrich, L. (2013, July 16). *The impact of digital tools on student writing and how writing is taught in schools.* Retrieved from http://pewinternet.org/Reports/2013/Teachers-technology-and-writing.

Roe, B. D., & Ross, E. P. (2006). *Integrating language arts through literature and thematic units.* New York: Allyn & Bacon.

Roskos, K. A., Tabors, P. O., & Lenhart, L. A. (2009). *Oral language and early literacy in preschool: Talking, reading, and writing.* Newark, DE: International Reading Association.

Rotella, C. (2013, September 15). *No child left untabled.* Retrieved from http://www.nytimes.com/2013/09/15/magazine/no-child-left-untabled.html?pagewanted=all&_r=0.

Sandberg, K. L., & Reschly, A. L. (2011). English learners: Challenges in assessment and the promise of curriculum-based measurement. *Remedial and Special Education, 32,* 144–154. doi:10.1177/0741932510361260

Schleppegrell, M. J. (2012). Academic language in teaching and learning: Introduction to the special issue. *The Elementary School Journal, 112*(3), 409–418.

Slavin, R. E. (1995). *Cooperative learning: Theory, research, and practice* (2nd ed.). Boston: Allyn & Bacon.

Staehr Fenner, D. (2016). Fair and square assessments for ELLs. *Educational Leadership, 73*(5). Retrieved from http://www.ascd.org/publications/educational-leadership/feb16/vol73/num05/Fair-And-Square-Assessments-for-ELLs.aspx.

Stanford University. (2013). *Key principles for ELL instruction.* Retrieved from http://ell.stanford.edu/sites/default/files/Key%20Principles%20for%20ELL%20Instruction%20with%20references_0.pdf.

Steelcase Education Solutions. (2014). *Active learning spaces: Insights, applications & solutions* (Vol 3). Retrieved from www.steelcase.com/educationsolutions.

Tharp, R. G., & Gallimore, R. (1991) *The instructional conversation: Teaching and learning in social activity* (Research Report 2). Santa Cruz, CA: National Center for Research on Diversity and Second Language Learning, University of California. Retrieved from http://scholarship.org/us/item/5th0939d.

Totten, S., Sills, T., Digby, A., & Russ, P. (1991). *Cooperative learning: A guide to research.* New York: Garland.

Tucker, C. (2012). *Blended learning in grades 4–12.* Thousand Oaks, CA: Corwin.

Tung, R., Uriarte, M., Diez, V., Gagnon, L., Stazesky, P., de los Reyes, E., et al. (2011). *Learning from consistently high performing and improving schools for English language learners in Boston Public Schools.* Boston: Center for Collaborative Education. Retrieved from http://files.eric.ed.gov/fulltext/ED540998.pdf.

Tyrell, J. (2011, October 18). Students pen middle school survival guide. *Newsday.* Retrieved from http://www.newsday.com/long-island/suffolk/students-pen-middle-school-survival-guide-1.3254803.

Vygotsky, L. S. (1978). *Mind in society: The development of higher psychological processes.* Cambridge, MA: Harvard University Press.

Whitby, T. (2014). *The relevant educator: How connectedness empowers learning.* Thousand Oaks, CA: Corwin.

WIDA. (2012). *English language proficiency standards.* Retrieved from www.wida.us.

WIDA. (2014). *Academic language and literacy.* Retrieved from https://www.wida.us/research/agenda/AcademicLanguage/index.aspx.

Wilder, P. (2010). *Teaching with multiple modalities: A strategy guide.* Retrieved from http://www.readwritethink.org/professional-development/strategy-guides/teaching-with-multiple-modalities-30101.html.

Willner, L., Rivera, C., & Acosta, B. D. (2009). Ensuring accommodations used in content assessments are responsive to English-language learners. *The Reading Teacher, 62*(8), 696–698. doi:10.1598/RT.62.8.8

Wolpert-Gawron, H. (2012, April 26). *Kids speak out on student engagement.* Retrieved from http://www.edutopia.org/blog/student-engagement-stories-heather-wolpert-gawron.

Wolsey, T. D., Lapp, D., & Fisher, D. (2010). Breaking the mold in secondary schools: Creating a culture of literacy. In A. Honigsfeld & A. Cohan (Eds.), *Breaking the mold of school instruction and organization* (pp. 9–16). New York: Rowman & Littlefield.

Wright, S. (2012). *Flipping Bloom's taxonomy*. Retrieved from https://shelley wright.wordpress.com/2012/05/29/flipping-blooms-taxonomy.

Zwiers, J. (2004–2005). The third language of academic English: Five key mental habits help English language learners acquire the language of school. *Educational Leadership, 62*(4), 60–63.

Zwiers, J. (2008). *Building academic language: Essential practices for content classrooms, grades 5–12.* San Francisco: Jossey-Bass.

Zwiers, J., & Crawford, M. (2009). How to start academic conversations. *Educational Leadership, 66*(7), 70–73.

Index